they are no...

BAS✝ARDS

in the
PULPIT

part 1

Practice
Higher Standard

Bastards in the Pulpit - Part 1
Copyright © 1998 by William Owens
william@higherstandard.net

Published by:
Higher Standard Publishers, LLC
www.higherstandardpublishers.com
Raleigh, NC

Owens, William, 1964
Bastards in the Pulpit
p. cm.
ISBN: 0-9658629-0-9
1. Owens, William 1964 2. Clergy
1st Printing 1998; 2nd Printing 2000; 3rd Printing 2002

All Scripture quotations are taken from the Holy Bible King James
Version

Cover Design Concept: W. Owens

Printed in the United States of America

TABLE OF CONTENTS

Chapter One

PERSPECTIVE 15

Chapter Two

EXPOSING THE PROBLEM 21

Chapter Three

WITHOUT FATHER 43

DEDICATION

The dedication of this book is to every born–again believer who loves Jesus with their whole being and desires revival within the hearts of God's people of every denomination, of every status and of every age.

The dedication of this book is to those who are aware of the hypocrisy that exists within the walls of the Church among leadership and have grown weary of diplomatic approaches.

The dedication of this book is to those who have been manipulated, set on the sideline and have experienced emotional hurt because of the religious deeds of men who claim a status of leadership that has not been ordained of heaven.

The dedication of this book is to those who believe that God has placed the seed of goodness in every person, but understands that when men no longer abide in Christ, they no longer can do good.

Ultimately, this book is dedicated to God who rejoices in His Word going forth for He longs to perform it on behalf of His faithful ones.

ACKNOWLEDGMENTS

To my wife, Selena, I honor you with the highest regard and respect, with none above you, save my Lord Jesus Christ and my Father God. You reveal my strength in your tenacity, and you feed my strength through your fixed gaze upon Jesus. You are truly one with me, for you have surrendered the interest of your life to the will of God. We, therefore, strive as one in fulfilling His mandate. Your endurance of trials and sufferings has purchased not only a rich welcome for you in the kingdom of God, but has birthed within you a treasure ready to be revealed to both men and women in the Body of Christ. Truly, God speaks through your meekness as a handmaiden of our risen Lord and King.

Thank you for typing and sharing in the labors of the following pages and for rejoicing with me when I rejoiced, and crying for me when I could not. I love you with a depth that only God could measure.

To my children Ryan, Tiffany, Bethany and David. Your contribution to me is not unnoticed. As I raise you to face your generation with the word of God in all boldness, each trial is a lesson that God uses to instruct me more perfectly in His ways. Your decision to follow my directions through obedience shall be rewarded. Those decisions that you make against my direction are used by God to shape you even more. I love you dearly, and am happy that God has smiled on your life by allowing me to usher you closer to His bosom.

Your patience in trials and sufferings that you endure along with me shall grow into a deeper understanding of God's ways, and a meaningful relationship with each other. Without the fire of trials, one has nothing but the chaff of men and a religion without power. I love you and respect your individuality. Thank you for allowing your father to pursue our Father.

Ryan, you are my oldest son and I am blessed to have you in my life. You have certainly endured the chastisement of my love and by the grace of God, you will be a son not only to me, but more so, to your heavenly Father in time to come. Certainly, you understand that the greatest reproach the devil would like to bring upon this work is to have you choose the way of a bastard. The devil is hideous in his pursuits but he is likewise defeated. I will never compromise my standard and love for Christ nor my commitment to be a father to you. In this, I am confident that He who has began a good work in you will complete it and that you will bring forth fruit unto the glory of God. Truly, son, apart from Him we can do nothing. I love you.

Certainly, God places people in your life who are members of our spiritual family. Such has He done through the friendship of Peggy Rayman who has provided feedback, editing and a due diligence to support this work that I am truly thankful for. Her scriptural and unbiased insights were a vital part of providing a balanced perspective to present such a work. Thank you, Peggy, for your service unto the Lord in helping me present this word to the Body of Christ.

FOREWARD

There was a man sent from God whose name was John. So was William Owens sent by God to us. After nearly forty years of existence on this planet, Evangelist William Owens has demonstrated growth and maturity in this bold and poignant book. As a messenger of special news from God's word to us, Owens must be commended for his courage to speak. This book is prophetic in the strong Hebraic sense of the word. The prophet in Hebrew is a "nabi" one who is a forthteller. One who is imbued with a "thus saith the Lord." Such a message cannot be gleaned from a prophetic conference, but rather from standing in the presence of the Lord waiting for instruction. Authentic prophets do not speak in their name. In fact, prophets are often perceived as strange breeds. They do not operate in flocks. They are often like eagles, loners, somewhere in the crags of lofty heights.

God will never allow the words of a prophet to fall to the ground. This book is a challenge to anyone who mounts the pulpit with their own self-serving greedy agenda. This author argues that "the process of chastisement begins as soon as we are born again into the family of God." I might add it continues in a more manifest way once we are called to ministry, The preacher who does not listen to God is similar to an "accident" about to happen. William Owens writes in a "no nonsense fashion." So did Ezekiel, Jeremiah and Amos prophesy judgment and deliverance to a backslidden people. Grace precedes judgment. In our time, judgment has begun in the House of God. Owens radically believes such judgment should begin in the pulpit.

This prophetic challenge is often not easy to digest. It is "bitter" in the mouth, but medicine for the spirit. To heed this warning is to begin a journey back to a place of integrity, power and intimacy with God. Owens is really begging the question, "Is Jesus really Lord of the church?" In order to save our communities, nation and the world, we must first be saved. There are outsiders who have lost respect for the church due to "loose living" and blatant immorality among the clergy. To heed this warning may be the key to regain such respect.

This book is radical, to say the least, so ought we to be. It gets to the heart of the matter. The Gospel is good news, bad news and indifferent news, it depends on the street where you are. If this book is on your street and has your name on it, read it, absorb it and obey it. Your ministry will improve. It is possible that one can be perceived as being great without really being good. This book challenges us not simply to be great preachers, but whole persons. The ancient psalmist wrote, "if the foundations be destroyed, what can the righteous do? These are dark days for the church, especially with scandals abounding within institutional churches. But we have the hope that sunshine always follows rain. Modern Baal worshipping, idolatrous, self-serving, self-indulgent greedy pupiteers must be challenged and called to accountability. "The axe must be laid to the root of the tree" is an admonition from Scripture, as the trumpet is sounded in Zion. This is a tough word for the church, that may even warrant undue criticism. However, it is hermeneutically sound,

biblically valid and radically engaging. The evangel has admonished us with a clarion call of urgency that really implies, "that if we listen to God, people will listen to us."

Leonard Lovett, Ph.D
January 2003

PREFACE

There is no other body like the Body of Christ, purchased with the blemish–free atoning blood of Jesus (Yeshua), Emmanuel, the Alpha and Omega, the Beginning and the End. I love God the Father, God (Yahweh) the Son and God the Holy Ghost with a passion that I have received of Him to have. I have a zeal and jealousy for Him and for whom He loves; the Body of Christ. I am a member of these "called out ones" from the defiled world in which we live. My zeal, however, is not blind, nor does it come by men. It is solely for God. Though I love the Body of Christ, my zeal is but for Christ Himself. None can have a zeal for Him and share it with another, for such is the danger of men.

We must seek, with a godly soberness, to understand the condition of this Body. We cannot see what we desire to see, but rather, the truth of what is really there. Despite the pain of the truth or the losses we encounter for truth's sake, if we love God, we must seek to understand His voice to the Church and simply submit. In doing so, He will forgive, heal, restore and empower to obey His commandments. For it is by obedience that He knows we love Him.

God is real. He does not cover up the sin of His people, nor does He care about the personalities of men who consider themselves someone, when they are altogether lighter than vanity. The Lord our God, who rides the thunders and rules in the affairs of men with and without their consent, desires truth in the inward parts and for the Body of Christ to remain spotless from the filth and iniquity that tarnishes it. Christ our Lord will not be mocked with modern day antidotes that excuse away the truth. Philosophies, motivationalism and all forms of "humanism", which appear in the form of "positive" ideologies, will not undermine His demand for holiness, obedience and separation from the world. Despite the peace and good that many are prophesying, they do so out of their own heart, which is not after God's heart. This fact is evident in one's fruit. We see the fruit of carnal philosophies that abounds in many of our pulpits. Impurities behind the pulpit are clearly in operation and identified by the deeds of those in front of the pulpit.

> *Jas 3:14–16 But if ye have bitter envying and strife in your hearts, glory not, and lie not against the truth. This wisdom descendeth not from above, but [is] earthly, sensual, devilish. For where envying and strife [is], there [is] confusion and every evil work.*

Finally, when the results of something are wrong, you must trace it to its source. Nothing is wrong with God. You must then look to the next element, namely His servants. Ah, my friend, there are bastards amongst the servants of the Most High. Truly, their time has come to a full bloom and inevitably, to God's judgment.

The Body of Christ has suffered at the hands of men at one time or another in all generations. Thus, we should not be surprised that our generation is in such a transitional state. These are men who have called themselves, taught themselves, ordained themselves, and chastised themselves. All that they have done or plan to do has been of themselves. It should come as no surprise that this is the very reason why they speak for themselves!

The Body of Christ must undergo massive heart surgery, for the venom of such men has attempted to tamper with the blood which cannot be tampered with. God is shaking that which is not after His counsel, His Spirit and His righteousness, and stabilizing that which is. Behold, it is upon you!

"Bastards in the Pulpit" is certainly not about faith that demands God to get something new for you. It is not about how to conduct a successful conference. It has nothing to do with being popular among people. It is far from man's idea of positive thinking. To many, it will appear to be in error and perhaps from the pit of hell. For those who use the grace of our Lord to practice lasciviousness, you will certainly be appalled. Perhaps the Spirit of the Lord will have mercy and allow you to see the soulishness of your heart. "Bastards in the Pulpit" is not written to sell a million but to please one - God!

"Bastards in the Pulpit" is a revelation of God's righteousness, God's holiness and God's wrath! It is an accountability check for those who have entered into His vineyard by some other way other than through the Good Shepherd. They are hirelings; men called by men, men made by men, men taught, selected and ruled by men. They are those who are called of God, but have refused His way, His chastisement and His will for their call. Such have gone to establish ministries bearing His name, yet void of His Spirit.

"Bastards in the Pulpit" is for the flock of Jesus Christ to check out the shepherd you are allowing to shepherd you. It should not come as a surprise for God's people to seek fruit of the under shepherd that you are allowing to lead you. It is to alert you to your responsibility to work out your own salvation in fear and trembling and to know your God. In this, you will not be tossed to and fro by every wind of doctrine, or by men who lie in wait to deceive.

Last of all, it is a warning before the return of Jesus Christ. A warning to return to our first love and to repent of the apostasy that has grasped the heart of God's shepherds. It is time for the prophets of Baal and Elijah to meet on top of mount Carmel and settle the issues of worship. Will it be Jehovah God or the traditions and commandment of men? Though we realize that until the Lord Himself descends from heaven to restore all things, we must be a voice of one crying in the wilderness in the city, in the state and in the nation. It is necessary that we publish abroad the wrong, the sin and the rebellion of God's people in and to our generation.

Woe is me if I silence my mouth with what He has given me to proclaim. The blood of many shall be required of me if I fail to articulate what He has inspired me to record. I covet your prayers for this mandate which is laid upon my life. I love the Lord along with those who call upon Him with a pure heart, and am fixed on the path that He has marked out for me and shall by no means draw back. I am fixed on heaven and my soul follows hard after Him. I admonish men to give Him the praise and reverence due Him, for not too many days hence we must stand before Him who is a Consuming Fire and give an account for our lives! Clean it up, clean it up, clean it up! Bastards in the pulpit are exposed!

When God has separated you to do a work for His kingdom, the reality of sacrifice of such a call goes far beyond what most Christians know or are willing to pay today. It demands time, even at the most inconvenient of times. It requires work and dedication when physical and mental capacities seem most strained. It consumes resources, that easily could be spent in other ways and places. Unfortunately, it inevitably costs friendships and relationships, either because the one called of God is misunderstood, or because the message he is required to give is rejected by those to whom he is sent.

As the author, I am the first to realize that this book, by its very title and subject matter, carries a word that is not popular and a theme that has been almost purposely ignored. It will not be accepted by some and may even stir resentment and anger among others. But please understand that what I have undertaken to address is neither meant to shock or offend by sensationalism, nor is it a matter of personal bitterness or revenge. It is truly not my desire to be offensive. Yet I also know that it is laid upon me to speak what God reveals and even though the truth might offend, I must never draw back from fear of the faces of men. This is indeed a heavy burden.

However, while I feel the weight of carrying out the burden my Lord has placed upon me, He has graciously placed around me those who love and support me. Indeed, I am blessed, and I most gladly give homage to them and the part they continue to play in the mandate that has been placed upon my life. They are the few who know me like no other and have seen my life day in and day out. Most of all, they love and respect me. When no one else is there, they are with me and they care. They are the ones, for better or for worse, who endure with me, regardless of the consequences. They are my family.

14

1

PERSPECTIVE

It is imperative for me to place into perspective this burden of the Lord that you, the reader, may fully understand this inspiration of God to me. Furthermore, it is essential that a solid, scriptural and spiritual foundation be laid that error may be avoided in both the inscription and its interpretation.

I am intensely aware of the title that this book bears. In like manner, I am aware that perhaps it is the reason that you were drawn to it. Allow me to set forth what "Bastards in the Pulpit" is about, and what it is not about; its goal, as well as the application of it.

WHAT IT IS ABOUT

This book is about men of God who have cast off the whole counsel of God, the holiness of God, and the requirements of God. In some ways or all ways, we all have gone astray and are found wanting in the ranks of leadership. Even in our apparent sin, it would be better to confess our sin, than to be in sin and call it righteousness! This book reveals why this has occurred. Also, it is a sober call to repent of the sin that those within the Body of Christ have yielded to. It is a prophetic warning to turn our hearts completely to the Lord and serve Him outside of the traditions of men or the burdens of denominationalism. It is about stirring men's conscience to repentance and breaking the fallow ground of the heart that is bent on fulfilling its lust, while imitating a relationship with Yahweh, our God and Savior.

Finally, it is a prophetic word of communicating truths to the leaders of our dispensation, coupled with a warning that God sees and knows all. It is a clear admonition to stop the games and repent. If there is any conscience left in those who would "seesaw" between two opinions and refuse to simply love the Lord or leave Him, then at least leave His heritage alone. For those who would question my credentials, let me be the first to say that I am by no means qualified by men, by education or by any right of my own to give this word. I did not ask God for it; He gave it to me. I am simply a "voice of one crying in the wilderness."

Start — His wrath is being kindled against those who say that they are apostles but are found liars (Rev. 2:2). It is an answer from the breath of the Almighty to the obvious forsaking of truth in the inward parts that has been exchanged for gain as being godly. This gain is of self-preservation and humanism in the realms of money, fame and pleasures of this life. It embraces philosophies, opinions and ideals that seek its own and the acceptance of others. We must conclude the issues of the heart as desperately wicked and to never be trusted without the watchful and loving eye of our Father. We are simply rejecting His Fatherhood and through fear and unbelief, yield to this condition of bastardship rather than sonship.

16

We must conclude that the heart, left to itself, will bring utter destruction. It is high time to believe the words of Christ lest we become prey for the enemy as he ensnares the world with the sticky threads of "New Age" philosophies. The words of Christ are, without a doubt, His and His alone. Truly, all others are antichrist, deceivers and impostors.

> *Joh 15:5,6 I am the vine, ye [are] the branches: He that abideth in me, and I in him, the same bringeth forth much fruit: for without me ye can do nothing. If a man abide not in me, he is cast forth as a branch, and is withered; and men gather them, and cast [them] into the fire, and they are burned.*

Ultimately, this book reveals why God has endured man's sin from the fall of Adam until the coming of Christ. We shall gain an understanding as to why God graciously forgave Adam and purposed on that day, (actually before the beginning of time), to crush the head of satan that He might be our God, and we might be His people. It is about Jesus Christ as God becoming Jesus Christ the Man only to ultimately become Jesus Christ the Savior, while as yet to become Christ Jesus, Lord of all. We yet await the consummation of all creation by which every knee shall bow and every tongue confess that Jesus Christ is Lord! We are being called to remembrance of the things that matter most, and through excessive means, God will capture excessive rebellion or cut off the sickness altogether (Rom. 11:22) The question that you and I must answer is, "will we submit or rebel even more?"

ITS GOAL

Obviously, the goal of this book is to awaken the consciousness of the people of God to obedience and to abandon the contemptible practices of the traditions of men.

Yet, the overall goal is far reaching. In fact, it reaches out of the realm of this life into the bliss of eternal life when we shall see Him as

He is. Thus, the goal is to snatch some out of hell's fire that they may experience entrance into heaven's gates.

> *Re 22:19 And if any man shall take away from the words of the book of this prophecy, God shall take away his part out of the book of life, and out of the holy city, and [from] the things which are written in this book.*

> *2Pe 2:21 For it had been better for them not to have known the way of righteousness, than, after they have known [it], to turn from the holy commandment delivered unto them.*

There is exists such a hell where devils torment beyond comprehension those who pollute God's truth. There will be a greater punishment because the truth was known but not obeyed. The core motivation of this book is for every reader to enter into heaven's courts, not by fire, but by the expectation of a rich welcome for doing service unto the Lord in complete righteousness.

The tone of this book is heavy. It is sometimes even harsh, but compared to the depth of hell for eternity, it is a sweet and kind word welcomed by those who will take heed.

WHAT IT IS NOT

This is not an expression of imbalance, or a result of too much Old Testament study. I have checked myself and continue to do so. In fact, I am open to be checked by all at any time. Even in my zeal with knowledge, I will not deny that there are some imperfections in this work. However, my desire and my intent are perfect even as I render my all to Him. Further, the only thing that can be labeled as "perfect" in any of this is that He be "perfectly" glorified.

This is not a result of rejection as some will assume. What man of God has not been rejected by God's people because of his stand for righteousness? We see that Samuel the prophet, (whose words never hit the ground), was displeased because he assumed that the people rejected him. God had to enlighten him that it was the Lord Himself that they had rejected, not Samuel (1 Samuel 8:6,7). Therefore, we understand that when rejection occurs because of truth, the messenger has not be rejected, but the One who sent him. It is a part of the call and such treatment was foretold (John 16:2). Such rejection is always purposed by God for us to taste those suffering for Christ's sake that has been reserved for us in order to truly know the message of our ministry through experience. Experience ensures that one does not assume ministry in the many pitfalls of religion and tradition that rest upon the approval of men.

> *Luke 6:26 Woe unto you, when all men shall speak well of you! for so did their fathers to the false prophets.*

This is not to show despite to God's leaders. Nevertheless, understand that when God's leaders no longer obey God's word, then such have shown despite to Him. When people are instructed to honor leadership and that leadership refuses to honor the very reasons for which they have been appointed a "leader", a person is not required to follow.

Openly, Peter declared, *"it is far better to obey God rather than man"*(Acts 5:29). Man becomes wicked when he esteems himself above correction, and deceives himself with the same error of Lucifer. It was pride that provoked Lucifer to believe that God had no right to make demands for worship. Even today, they believe the same. Paul said it with simplicity:

19

1Cor 11:1 Be ye followers of me, even as I also am of Christ.

What more could be said to properly introduce this prophetic exhortation and warning to God's people from one who is born for this reason yet not afraid? I was born to fulfill the will of God by the Spirit of God through the mercy of God. I am challenged beyond measure to accomplish it by His grace, unqualified by the standards of many, yet ordained before my father knew my mother.

My words would be that I love God and, oh, how I love His people, for I am of this fold even as you are, and this word is to me before it is to anyone. If I do not say it, the blood of many will rest upon me. And if I say it and do not obey it, I will be a castaway having yet preached to others and not obeyed the word myself. My love is not my own, for such love is unable to work the righteousness of God. My love is of God and therefore, I will not rejoice in iniquity but rejoice in the truth!

This introduction is not intended to soften the word of the Lord for fear, but to enable His word to be as effective as I am able to make it. I shall not fear man, for what can man do to me?

2 EXPOSING THE PROBLEM

Ecc 3:3 A time to kill, and a time to heal; a time to break down, and a time to build up;

Ecc 3:7 A time to rend, and a time to sew; a time to keep silence, and a time to speak;

Be sure of this; the time has come to break down, and it is the responsibility of those who hear the word of the Lord to speak. For too long, we have justified not speaking the judgments of God. Through the lust of the flesh, we have yielded to humanism and thus to withholding the full counsel of the Lord. We have considered the hearts of men over the heart of God. We fear the face of mere clay that has no power rather than fearing God who holds all power! Through wrestling against His Holy Word, we have even justified our cowardice at preaching the full counsel of God.

In essence, we have rebelled from telling the whole truth and nothing but the truth. We have gone astray and are blinded by our waywardness. We have sinned and will not confess it.

> *Jer 8:6 I hearkened and heard, but they spoke not aright: no man repented him of his wickedness, saying, What have I done? every one turned to his course, as the horse rusheth into the battle.*

There is a problem, and the leadership of the Body of Christ must face it with humility, courage and godly fear. Yes, the Lord has a voice, even today, and those who obey Him will proclaim His whole word with the power of His conviction behind them.

> *Jer 23:28 The prophet that hath a dream, let him tell a dream; and he that hath my word, let him speak my word faithfully. What is the chaff to the wheat? saith the LORD.*

> *2 Cor 4:2 But have renounced the hidden things of dishonesty, not walking in craftiness, nor handling the word of God deceitfully; but by manifestation of the truth commending ourselves to every man's conscience in the sight of God.*

In the same way that Adam yielded to the deception of the knowledge of good and evil and then blamed God for the very wife He gave him, we have yielded to fulfilling our own righteousness so as to avoid our responsibility to simply obey. The responsibility of the watchman is to tell the truth! As simple as this may seem, failure after failure prevails. The problem is that the priests and the prophets have profaned the word of the Lord, and their venom has poisoned many. When the Church ignores the truth, they have, in essence, ignored God. The more that we accept this and refuse to speak out, the more sin and rebellion settles in and fixes themselves upon the heart of their victim. Thus, the heart becomes unable to provide clean blood to the rest of the body. The result is seen from the head to the feet. We are especially affected in the eyes because we fail to see the error of our ways and then we fail to hearken to the truth even though it is shouted from the mountain top. Why?

Ecc 8:11 Because sentence against an evil work is not executed speedily, therefore the heart of the sons of men is fully set in them to do evil.

The "Eve" that we point to today is an array of weak and beggarly idols. They are excuses as old as man. When Eve was on the spot, she passed the blame onto the serpent. In like manner, somehow, some demon has been tagged with the blame of causing us to yield to the spirit of humanism, philosophies, and even doctrines that are clearly New Age. In doing so, we deny the Lord who is our God. However, when we get down to the core of our motives, we are not really blaming Eve, or the devil, or the shadows on the wall. We have said along with Adam, "That woman that YOU (God) gave me." Yes, we are accusing God of not restraining us from rebelling against Him!

King Saul was a prime example of fear and his failure was fixed:

1Sam 15:24 And Saul said unto Samuel, I have sinned: for I have transgressed the commandment of the LORD, and thy words: because I feared the people, and obeyed their voice.

Exposing the problem is not a choice as servants of God. It is a mandate, an irrevocable order. A command bearing a weight of responsibility that extends into eternity. It comes down to perceiving a true man of God in the pulpit from a bastard in the pulpit. It comes down to knowing the difference between one who has been purged from self-interests, political agendas, fear of faces, and hidden sins, to one who justifies his sins because of grace. By justifying his sin, he does despite to God's grace.

23

Jer 23:22 But if they had stood in my counsel, and had caused my people to hear my words, then they should have turned them from their evil way, and from the evil of their doings.

Eph 5:11 And have no fellowship with the unfruitful works of darkness, but rather reprove them.

2 Tim 4:2 Preach the word; be instant in season, out of season; reprove, rebuke, exhort with all longsuffering and doctrine.

It is obvious that the problem cannot be isolated to any single issue, therefore, it must be realized that the problem consists of many things. Democracy is flourishing within God's Church rather than theocracy. There are problems and God knows how to handle them. There is a breach in the dam, and God has stepped down from heaven to fix it. Men are attempting to control God's heritage, God's program and God's preordained will which is ordered after the counsel of Himself, by Himself and for Himself.

Too often, we believe in telling some of God's truth and not all of God's truth. We are quick to declare, "Without faith, it is impossible to please God", but seldom declare, "Without holiness, no man shall see God!"

Heb 12:14 Follow peace with all [men], and holiness, without which no man shall see the Lord:

In our sick theology, we somehow believe that the terrible God of the Old Testament is not relevant for our generation. We have misrepresented His love as being without order and His grace as a reason to sin more than a reason *not* to sin. We have committed a double offense of adultery, doing despite to His love and His grace. Jesus did not come to do away with the law and the prophets, but to fulfill them.

24

Matt 5:17 Think not that I am come to destroy the law, or the prophets: I am not come to destroy, but to fulfill.

We have set up camps of rebellion and ministries of pleasure in declaring how good God is, and not how just, holy and righteous He is. In our over zealous love for "faith", we have erected a monument to it. We have relinquished our families, marriages and treasures to worship its supposed power. FAITH! The devil has used the things of God to pollute the people of God. We have looked to the heathen and desired their dainties and their democracy; the rule of man, over the rule of God; theocracy!

What difference is our "faith" from the witches, fortune tellers, soothesayers, or 900–number liars of our time? Is it that we hold the Bible, speak in tongues, sing worship songs, proclaim, "Jesus is Lord", and follow all manner of religious exercises? Is this what makes our faith different than that of the heathen, the publicans, or the sinner?

Dare we hide behind "relationships" with God, which are built on the letter of His word, but not the Spirit of it? Dare we turn the pages of His holy writ to support our image of faith, our god of hope, our ticket to lust, and burn after the imaginations of our own hearts?

I am full of His word and cannot withhold what He has spoken. Bear with me, those who love Jesus, and rejoice in the truth and not iniquity. John spoke it well, did he not?

Matt 3:8 Bring forth therefore fruits meet for repentance:

The issue is not faith as the stubborn human heart would want to believe. It is fruit! Oh, yes, we speak of faith, but not the fruit of the Spirit. Instead, we glory in the fruit of "faith"; cars, houses, revelation, church membership and such things that provide pleasure for our flesh. When these are sought after at the expense of sonship and truth, they are vain. They will only pierce our hearts through with sorrow and cause our faith to shipwreck upon the shores of deception. Witch doc-

25

tors and sorcerers are manipulators of the spirit world. Certainly, we, as the people of God, are aware that He will not be ruled or controlled by repetitive words that are fiercely believed by one or even a thousand. God is after one will - His.

We have refused to expose the problem. Of course, we talk about the problem and offer solutions that are after the futile knowledge of man. However, we choose to partake in society's idea of righteousness and in time, we become friends of politicians and popular celebrities believing that their "image" will provide the missing link. We offer to be reconciled to others despite our broken relationship with God. We align ourselves with foreign parties whose agenda is one world order. We feel "secure" in the freedoms that a government of men gives us, while ignoring the freedom that God, head of all governments has given us. But God shall raise up many voices! He will do this to declare, expose and make known the sin of His people. He shall stand behind and prove His own word by His own power that reaches within the heart and reveals all the hidden agendas of His people.

> *Jer 23:29 Is not my word like as a fire? saith the LORD; and like a hammer that breaketh the rock in pieces?*

> *Heb 4:12,13 For the word of God is quick, and powerful, and sharper than any two edged sword, piercing even to the dividing asunder of soul and spirit, and of the joints and marrow, and is a discerner of the thoughts and intents of the heart. Neither is there any creature that is not manifest in his sight: but all things are naked and opened unto the eyes of him with whom we have to do.*

A TIME TO TEAR DOWN AND A TIME TO SPEAK

Does the Church of the Living God know what time it is? It is important that you see by the Spirit! Do not look, but see. Pray that the eyes of your understanding might be enlightened to see and hear the Spirit of God! Oh, how it burns in the depths of my soul at the apostasy, and yet we say, "What apostasy?" We sin, and we say, "What

> *Rev 3:17 Because thou sayest, I am rich, and increased with goods, and have need of nothing; and knowest not that thou art wretched, and miserable, and poor, and blind, and naked:*

There are men leading the Church who are not after God's heart. They have crept in unawares. It was foreordained that such would become a reality in each generation. Why, then, do we become stunned when we see the day upon us?

> *Jude 1:4 For there are certain men crept in unawares, who were before of old ordained to this condemnation, ungodly men, turning the grace of our God into lasciviousness, and denying the only Lord God, and our Lord Jesus Christ.*

As you were ordained unto life, they have been ordained unto condemnation. Even as Judas Iscariot was ordained to fulfill the righteousness of God, there are men, ungodly men, who turn the blood of our covenant with God into lasciviousness, and by doing so, deny the only Lord God, our Lord Jesus Christ.

The problem has been classified presumptuously as weak faith, not enough confession and insufficient worship with all of your heart. Maybe it is your tithe and offering. Are you under leadership? You are not a member of a church that speaks in tongues? You do not speak in tongues? Enough is enough!

27

Rather than speaking out against the sins of God's people, we instead run for office attempting, through our foolish wisdom, to turn the agenda of this world into the agenda of God's world. Though Daniel ruled in the high courts, He did so by God's agenda. His purpose was to uphold the word of the Lord, not to campaign for heaven on earth.

> *Dan 6:4,5 Then the presidents and princes sought to find occasion against Daniel concerning the kingdom; but they could find none occasion nor fault; for as much as he was faithful, neither was there any error or fault found in him. Then said these men, We shall not find any occasion against this Daniel, except we find it against him concerning the law of his God.*

Their only hope was to find occasion against Daniel concerning his God. Daniel either had to compromise to keep this position with men, or stand to keep his position with God. Those who have compromised to keep the place of the popular, the rich, the affluent and the well dressed have lost their place with God! You should have rather chosen the lion's den whether or not you were consumed. It would be better to suffer affliction with the people of God than to enjoy the pleasures of sin for a season (Heb. 11:25). But you did not! Through the lust of covetousness, you esteemed the riches of Egypt greater than the reproach of Christ (v.26). You have more desire for the acceptance of men than for the acceptance of God.

28

> *Mt 16:23 But he turned, and said unto Peter, Get thee behind me, Satan: thou art an offence unto me: for thou savourest not the things that be of God, but those that be of men.*

Indeed, we all struggle with this temptation, however, God is able to make us true to stand against the forms and fashions of men. It is not too late to repent of this doubt, fear and rebellion against God's faithfulness and righteousness.

Daniel was ready to die a most horrible death, yet men today believe that the demands of God have changed. Humanism once again has caused us to believe that God does not require those who grace the pulpits of this country to cry aloud and spare not. It is really quite simple. As men of God, we have buckled under the pressures of upholding His standard. Though we are yet alone and there be thousands against us, we cannot draw back, for truly, His soul will have no pleasure in those who do. He will never leave nor forsake us. We foolishly assume that it is because of the dispensation of grace that God is not as concerned with His righteousness, His holiness, and His Word. Thus, many have utilized grace as a license to work iniquity or as a reason to ignore it. We must not forget that the whole counsel of God declares that His word shall not return to Him void but will accomplish His righteousness!

Bastards in the pulpit are sure to face serious times of chastisement, abasement and much loss unless, with haste, they repent!

A TIME TO BREAK DOWN

There is a definite purpose for the proclamation of this utterance. It is the beginning of the shaking in the house of God that many beforehand have prophesied would come. It is breaking down the control and manipulation of God's people by polluted and weak-hearted leadership. Regardless of who they are, where they are, or what they have done, it is time for God to be true and for men to be a liar. The breaking down will allow every man's work to be made manifest of what sort it is. Is it wood or stubble, or gold and silver? We must not have respect of persons, for the truth will shine and such light will bring revelation of who we really are by the fruit that we bear.

This book will expose persons who are not declaring the whole counsel of God and accompanying that counsel with a life-style of holiness and a zeal for obedience. Though direct, it is not without love, not without mercy and certainly not without grace. Though serious in tone, this book is all about life and that life will only be found in God through His Son, Jesus Christ who is King. His government is upon His shoulders and those who herald His message must do so in fear, for He is Judge. This alone must be our fear and dread.

This book seeks to break down the idle, hopeless and lustful hopes that many of God's people have turned to. They have sought the pleasures of this life, this world, and vain religion to replace the intimate, personal and heaven bound relationship that He demands; a relationship that He died to make possible. The very thrust of this relationship was and is sonship. If we are not sons, we are bastards, for He will only declare His sons as His own.

This message will hopefully break down traditions established by prejudices that range from bigotry, male and female chauvinism, worship of doctrines and all such commandments and ordinances of men that make the word of God of none effect. Such traditions block the mind of God's people from seeking Him and endeavoring to hear His voice. These traditions are expensive and costly to God's people. They place financial burdens upon His sheep that robs them of the liberty and joy that belongs to their family. Excessive demands and pursuits are centered on a building and fleshly works that are measured merely by dollars and cents. While finances are ordained of God and certainly have a purpose, we must remember that the real ministries are those that are embodied in the lives of people who God has anointed to declare the whole counsel of His word. More than money, true ministries thrive on obedience and seeing the glory of the Lord revealed at the acceptance of the pure word of God.

This message seeks to break down systems that are designed for men not to be men. As a result of these systems, men never become fathers who learn by watching their father. Furthermore, this message will confront leadership that operates through manipulation and inhibits those who desire the things of God from pressing into them. Such ministries operate only to expand their borders throughout this country by associating and develop relationships that are in keeping with manipulative ideas. Isaiah declared a woe to them that is worth repeating to our generation.

> *Is 5:8 Woe unto them that join house to house, that lay field to field, till there be no place, that they may be placed alone in the midst of the earth!*

Jesus declared it as well:

> *Matt 23:13 But woe unto you, scribes and Pharisees, hypocrites! for ye shut up the kingdom of heaven against men: for ye neither go in yourselves, neither suffer ye them that are entering to go in.*

To ensure such warped success, those who operate from a core of guile must keep the truth from abounding. They must not allow the Word of God to be hurled with power, for then the people are free to worship the Lord in true liberty. It is time to break down the system designed to make merchandise of God's heritage.

2 Pet 2:3 And through covetousness shall they with feigned words make merchandise of you: whose judgment now of a long time lingereth not, and their damnation slumbereth not.

It is time to expose the feigned words that are concocted to rape the people of God spiritually and financially. The Twentieth Century New Testament translates it as such:

"In their covetousness, they will try to make you a source of profit by their fabrications."

The Modern Language Bible expresses it this way:

"Motivated by greed, they will exploit you with their counterfeit arguments."

It is time for holiness to be restored to God's people. Through yielding to the doctrine of devils, Scriptures are presented without qualification and regard to God's character, God's person and God's standard. With soulish, pious motives men declare, "By grace we are saved, through faith and not by works", but fail to say:

Rom 11:22 Behold therefore the goodness and severity of God: on them which fell, severity; but toward thee, goodness, if thou continue in his goodness: otherwise thou also shalt be cut off.

Indeed, we run to find shelter under the word (letter) of God, but not under God Himself.

John 5:39, 40 Search the Scriptures; for in them ye think ye have eternal life: and they are they which testify of me. And ye will not come to me, that ye might have life.

We attempt to find security in partial truth, and thus we are naked, blind and found wanting. We rest the hope of our salvation upon a letter…

John 10:28 And I give unto them eternal life; and they shall never perish, neither shall any man pluck them out of my hand.

…but refuse to rest it upon obedience, for it is not the hearers of the law that are justified before God, but the doers of the law (Rom. 2:13).

What more shall I say that must be broken down? Time would fail me. Paper and ink would be found no more to list the atrocities of God's people towards Him. Prevalent ones consist of:

- Christian psychology yields more respect than the Holy Ghost.

- Seminary accomplishments are esteemed more highly than God's appointed leadership.

- Fathers are not raising their sons; sons are mocking their fathers.

- Harlotry and fornication among men and women in the church is obvious and yet not confronted.

- Men seek relationships of the flesh with each other rather than a relationship in the Spirit for God's glory.

- Networking has replaced prayer, fasting and yielding to God's direction.

It is not knowing God through a personal relationship and His word that gains an advantage today. Rather, it is knowing the personalities of men that we trust and depend on for promotion. Does not Scripture declare who promotes?

> *Ps 75:6, 7 For promotion [cometh] neither from the east, nor from the west, nor from the south. But God [is] the judge: he putteth down one, and setteth up another.*

"Well, God uses men," we say. But we fail to realize that He does so because He chooses to. He could very well send a donkey or a chicken to confirm His prophecy. Have we forgotten that the rocks could be considered heirs to Abraham and, if permitted by God, would cry out, "Hosanna, Hosanna, blessed be the name of the Lord?"

> *Isa 2:22 Cease ye from man, whose breath is in his nostrils: for wherein is he to be accounted of?*

> *Job 25:6 How much less man, that is a worm? and the son of man, which is a worm?*

This book is written by a mandate from the God of heaven, earth, and of all that was, that is, and that shall be. I am a man most miserable if I fail to declare that there are bastards in the pulpits of America!

A TIME TO SPEAK

"It's not time, honey." "Be patient, brother. God will bring it to pass." "When it is time, you will know it." Does anyone know what time it is? By the Spirit of the Living God, I do!

> *Psa 119:126 It is time for thee, LORD, to work: for they have made void thy law.*

In our hypocritical, super religious way, we know when it is going to rain, we know when to ask for the tithe and offering, but as those who grace the pulpit, we have forgotten to declare the whole counsel of God's word. These are bastards, not true sons, or sons who have rejected the purging hand of God their Father.

Heb 12:8 But if ye be without chastisement, whereof all are partakers, then are ye bastards, and not sons.

John 15:2 Every branch in me that beareth not fruit he taketh away: and every branch that beareth fruit, he purgeth it, that it may bring forth more fruit.

Do not mistake this as a book of a man's opinion. That would indeed provide an excuse for rejecting this word. It certainly will not be perfect in its presentation, yet the contents are based on truth and will be proven to be valid by scriptural support based on love, not condemnation.

This is a book based on God's counsel and God's truth, and that with power. If you are born of God, His Spirit rejoices in you because truth is being declared. If you are not born of God, you are convicted, and it condemns you, for God's wrath is upon you. You will either find sackcloth and ashes and repent, or say that I, the writer, am in error. *But do not say that it is a man's opinion!*

It is time to speak, to lift up your voice, and say what God is saying. Enough of borderline religion! People appear confused in many churches today. In some circles, it is even difficult to determine if it is the Gospel of Jesus Christ being preached and taught, or if it is a mere class on spiritualism and motivation.

The Apostle Paul said:

1Cor 2:4 And my speech and my preaching was not with enticing words of man's wisdom, but in demonstration of the Spirit and of power:

1Cor 4:20 For the kingdom of God is not in word, but in power.

It is time to speak and not discuss! Time to choose between the worship of Baal (your religion, your tradition, your denomination, or idols of doctrine) and the One True God—Yahweh, I AM, the Alpha and Omega, the Beginning and the End. This choice is crucial but necessary. It causes everyone on every level to give an account of what they have declared for years.

In speaking this word, our pulpits will be challenged. A standard will be raised and thus the conscience of God's people convicted of the truth that is being uttered. This spoken word must go forth that peradventure, according to the mercy of God, we will witness a great return to declaring the truth with a standard that is without fear and respect of persons. Through this word, judgment will be experienced within the heart of God's people. This judgment will also come upon those works that have been built after the flesh and after the commandments of men. More respect has been given to denominations and agendas of men than to heavenly agendas.

Some who hear this word and see the effect it causes upon God's people will respond in protest as the truth is being revealed. As well, this word will arouse those who are found in a state of rejecting God's chastisement to fight against those who herald such bold truth, but they will not prevail.

It is time to speak, ye mighty men of valor. You have sought the Lord, but have been rejected by men.

It is time to speak, those of you who burn with the fire of God's word, for you are weary of containing it.

However, first and foremost, you must speak to yourself of your own sin and rebellion. You have to confront your own fears. Man of God, you must speak to your wife, and correct her with the wisdom of

36

God, and love her with the love of Christ! It is imperative that we first remove the beam in our own eye that we may see clearly to remove the speck from our brother's eye. Even in our imperfections, Christ's love is able to perfect us. Our priority is to be found ready when the Lord comes forth and requires an answer. <u>It is time to be sober and to understand that the times of peace are times to prepare for war.</u>

> *Eph 5:15–17 See then that ye walk circumspectly, not as fools, but as wise, Redeeming the time, because the days are evil. Wherefore be ye not unwise, but understanding what the will of the Lord [is].*

I say to the woman of God, you must *demonstrate* the oracles of God to your husband *without words,* for you will encourage him to search for the Lord if he knows Him not. By doing so, you will reveal, through your life, the things of God that cannot be heard but only seen. Exemplifying this in everyday living is more powerful than giving him a sermon on why he should go to church. As a woman, you have the God given ability to touch your husband in the depth of his being unlike any other human being. It is through you that God will touch him. Through your demonstration of love, he will see Christ.

Many of the frustrations that wives experience are a result of not operating in the protocols of God's kingdom. Until women and wives understand this principle, what they do understand will only operate in a limited capacity rather than it working the full righteousness of God's intended design. The principle is this; you cannot change a man—only God can. Follow the instructions below and you will reap the favor of God. Follow your own emotions and the advice of the world, and you will reap strife.

> *1Pet 3:1–4 Likewise, ye wives, be in subjection to your own husbands; that, if any obey not the word, they also may*

37

without the word be won by the conversation of the wives;
While they behold your chaste conversation coupled with fear.
Whose adorning let it not be that outward adorning of plait-
ing the hair, and of wearing of gold, or of putting on of ap-
parel; But let it be the hidden man of the heart, in that which
is not corruptible, even the ornament of a meek and quiet
spirit, which is in the sight of God of great price.

Parents, you must speak correction to your children. Abraham was blessed because God knew he would teach his seed to know the Lord. In fact, it was *because* Abraham commanded his children and his household after him that God destined he would become the father of faith. This demonstrates that as it takes time to produce sons, it also takes time to produce bastards.

Ge 18:18, 19 Seeing that Abraham shall surely become a
great and mighty nation, and all the nations of the earth shall
be blessed in him? For I know him, that he will command his
children and his household after him, and they shall keep the
way of the LORD, to do justice and judgment; that the LORD
may bring upon Abraham that which he hath spoken of him.

I speak to those who grace the place of utterance in the name of the Almighty. Some have been given a word, and yet it comes forth void in their own life. It is time to speak to ourselves what we have been speaking to others. Only then will we be anointed to speak from the mountain tops the demands of Him who is a Consuming Fire, and He who sets up kings and brings them down. We shall be inspired by Him who reveals deep things and sees in the dark as in the light because the light dwelleth with Him, He does not dwell with it (Dan. 2:21–22).

It is time. Furthermore, I shall speak that there are bastards in the pulpit and the hand of the Lord is lifting their skirts to reveal the shame of those who have tampered with the things of God that sim-

38

ply cannot be tampered with. It is time for the repercussion of decisions to be experienced for the godly and for the ungodly, as well as for the obedient and disobedient.

APPLICATION

The application of truth is the pinnacle of serving the Lord. It is through application that the power of God's word is released. Confession is not enough. God's word penetrates every layer of existence and forces itself upon the scene of life. Until we apply the word by faith and by the Spirit through relationship with God by Jesus Christ, failure and confusion will abound.

As you read the following pages, an understanding of application will enable the reader to better understand the author's heart.

We are quite aware of the spiritual warfare that we face, for all the activity of our earthly life is a direct result of our successes and failures in the spiritual realm. If you have not faced the principalities, powers, rulers of the darkness of this world and spiritual wickedness in high places, any form of ministry is surface and has no lasting effect. In fact, if it does not touch the core of the problem in the spiritual air, progress has not been made. "For we wrestle not against flesh and blood, but against principalities, against powers, against the rulers of the darkness of this world, against spiritual wickedness in high places" (Eph. 6:12).

This book of warning and exhortation must be applied spiritually in every sense of the word. As Jesus said:

John 6:63 It is the spirit that quickeneth; the flesh profiteth nothing: the words that I speak unto you, they are spirit, and they are life.

If interpreted by the counsel of man through mere application of the emotions and by human opinion, then this book will be interpreted as a criticism of men, rather than a warning, a word of exhortation and a word of God's love and honor for truth and righteousness.

If we really probed into the words of Jesus, we would find that He talks of the issue of wolves, hypocrites and all men who appear to be righteous, but inwardly are full of dead men's bones and all uncleanliness. It is written:

> *Matt 23:27–28 Woe unto you, scribes and Pharisees, hypocrites! for ye are like unto whited sepulchres, which indeed appear beautiful outward, but are within full of dead men's bones, and of all uncleanness. Even so, ye also outwardly appear righteous unto men, but within ye are full of hypocrisy and iniquity.*

America acknowledges an astounding 80% Christian loyalty, yet people are leaving churches Sunday after Sunday unmoved, unconverted, and unpersuaded of the God that they profess to know. We have tried to remedy this condition with formulas from prayer to fasting, church growth workshops, marketing campaigns and many similar efforts. However, such attempts have failed to answer the real problem. Though it appears that we have increased our church membership it is not true according to Barna Research. What has occurred is referred to as a lateral movement in that smaller churches are closing down, while people are moving toward bigger churches. The only valid question that needs to be answered is, "Are we increasing Christ membership rather than what appears to be "Church" membership?" We have developed fruitful programs but no faithful prayer. We have established favored democracy and thus rejected faithful theocracy - the rule of God!

40

While this is true in our generation of Christendom, it is also certain that building the kingdom of God is paramount, necessary and commanded. Having protocol insures godly order. Such needed structures are without question, however, when leadership advances any agenda no matter how warranted and yet they themselves are not articulating the Fatherhood of God through preaching and teaching as the Spirit gives utterance, supported by a life-style that is commendable before men, their motives are to be weighed.

By the Spirit of God, I am beseeching those who have eyes to see and ears to hear, with outstretched arms and even in tears, to apply these truths by the Spirit and not by the letter! For those who will yet fail to see the truth and attempt to find your comfort in trying to fix it, so be it. As the Word declares, some have been given over to the lie that holds the truth in unrighteousness.

> *Rom 1:25 Who changed the truth of God into a lie, and worshipped and served the creature more than the Creator, who is blessed for ever. Amen.*

I am going through great pains to ensure that the truth of this issue is correctly presented and that the application is understood to the end that God may be glorified and His people would repent of the sins that we have committed against Him.

There is no form of application for such; only a prayer of extreme mercy that, by God's sovereign power and incomprehensible love, those who are in such a state would stop and see what manner of God they are playing with. Stop! Fall on your faces and repent until God forgives. Stop! You would rather be found a thief in another man's vineyard than God's. Stop - just stop for your own eternal sake.

"Lord, You are a Consuming Fire. You know the thoughts of the righteous and the thoughts of the wicked. You rule and super-rule. You establish kings and You dethrone them as well. Man is but a worm, and the nations but a drop in the bucket.

I pray to You, Lord, that Your purpose be fulfilled in this book. I have obeyed and will obey. Confirm Your word, O Lord, with power. Shake the hearts of Your people that they may know this is true. Convict those in sin to judge themselves, that they be not judged of You. Confound and confuse the deceitfulness of man's imagination and bring it to nought. Ignite the faithful to arise to the battle, and make their faces like flint. May Your love for Your people radiate through us to one another, for by this men shall know that we are Your disciples and by this, we shall not be tossed to and fro by every wind of doctrine as we abide in Your word and walk in the truth.

O Lord, anoint those who utter Your word and have been called to declare the oracles of God to lift up their voices and spare not. To those who have yielded to the doctrine of devils and have exchanged the truth for a lie and therefore, have refused Your sonship, may they peradventure find a place of repentance less they heap unto themselves wrath against the day of wrath. Thy will be done, O Lord. Amen and Amen."

WITHOUT FATHER

Deut 32:6 Do ye thus requite the LORD, O foolish people and unwise? is not he thy father that hath bought thee? hath he not made thee, and established thee?

Heb 12:9 Furthermore we have had fathers of our flesh which corrected us, and we gave them reverence: shall we not much rather be in subjection unto the Father of spirits, and live?

A BASTARD:

a. An illegitimate child, but not necessarily a child born out of wedlock. The term could refer to offspring of an incestuous union or of a marriage that was prohibited (Lev. 18:6–20).

b. Illegitimate children were not permitted to enter the assembly of the Lord (Deut. 23:2).

c. According to Hebrews 12:8, those who do not have the disciplines of the Lord are illegitimate children (Holman Bible Dictionary p.156).

The word "bastard" appears in the Bible only 3 times with one of those appearances found in the New Testament. It denotes a streamline thought that causes the human nature to become very uncomfortable as there is no father, no source, no identity, no protector, or no sustaining power, which emanates from God. It depicts a horrible position that one is born into naturally or placed into spiritually. It is not a natural flow of life. Something has happened to cause this hideous spirit to manifest itself, and it must be dealt with by truth and that by the Holy Ghost which confronts the sin and cleanses the offender, if they submit themselves to the only Advocate who can cleanse; Jesus Christ.

This reality of being without father is not new. Perhaps it is new to our generation, but it has existed in the world since Adam cast off the restraints of His Father; God. As a result, he was separated from the life that was only in God and placed under the law. Being under the law did not make Adam a bastard. The law was a result of disobeying God's command of not eating of the forbidden fruit. Therefore, we understand that Adam was being chastised for his wrong. Should he disobey the law, then he would have been a bastard; one who refused to follow God's direction and experience the necessary discipline to be conformed back to God's character and ways.

> *Heb 12:10–11 For they verily for a few days chastened us after their own pleasure; but he for our profit, that we might be partakers of his holiness. Now no chastening for the present seemeth to be joyous, but grievous: nevertheless afterward it yieldeth the peaceable fruit of righteousness unto them which are exercised thereby.*

44

The very pulse of man's heart is to find his own way and take glory in self–preservation. This is the spirit that has caused putrefying sores, wounds and bruises to appear on the heads and feet of our nations and our homes. There is no country without excuse, no not one. From the Bahamas to California, around the Pacific then to Japan, there are sores upon the heads of those who have cast off the chastisement of their Heavenly Father, God, through Jesus Christ alone.

HOW IT HAPPENS

It is imperative that a clear and concise understanding be given as to how this position of being without father occurs. While it is clear that the work of salvation is a work of grace by faith, such a work demands that we conduct ourselves to show forth this grace that we have received of God. There is a necessary tension between grace and faith. That tension is termed, "working out your salvation." Not the workings of our own righteousness, but of His Spirit through us to bear fruit that testifies that His grace is present in this faith.

> *Eph 2:8-10 For by grace are ye saved through faith; and that not of yourselves: it is the gift of God: Not of works, lest any man should boast. For we are his workmanship, created in Christ Jesus unto good works, which God hath before ordained that we should walk in them.*

The process of chastisement begins as soon as we are born again into the family of God. As soon as the Spirit of God takes residence in us, He begins to develop the conditions by which we can bear the fruit that glorifies Him. Any branch that is in the vine and refuses to bring forth fruit will be purged by the Father.

> *Jo 15:2 Every branch in me that beareth not fruit he taketh away: and every branch that beareth fruit, he purgeth it, that it may bring forth more fruit.*

I will review 7 reasons how the position of a bastard occurs:

1. Eternal Security

Before I proceed to establish the fact of chastisement, I discern it wise for me to first of all address the issue of "eternal salvation" as it is labeled. Supposedly, this means that no matter what we do, our salvation is assured. When presented in this fashion, such a statement is candidly wrong. It cannot be supported upon Scripture nor will it validate the character of God and His holiness or the entire force of His plan of redemption. Though I could address this issue at length, I will focus on the present topic. Here are a few Scriptures to substantiate why this is not possible. I will then communicate why and how this is an important to understand what a bastard is.

> *Ro11:21,22 For if God spared not the natural branches, take heed lest he also spare not thee. Behold therefore the goodness and severity of God: on them which fell, severity; but toward thee, goodness, if thou continue in his goodness: otherwise thou also shalt be cut off.*
>
> *Heb 2:1-3 Therefore we ought to give the more earnest heed to the things which we have heard, lest at any time we should let them slip. For if the word spoken by angels was stedfast, and every transgression and disobedience received a just recompence of reward; How shall we escape, if we neglect so great salvation; which at the first began to be spoken by the Lord, and was confirmed unto us by them that heard him;*
>
> *2 Pet 2:20-21 For if after they have escaped the pollutions of the world through the knowledge of the Lord and Saviour Jesus Christ, they are again entangled therein, and overcome, the latter end is worse with them than the beginning. For it had been better for them not to have known the way of righteousness, than, after they have known it, to turn from the holy commandment delivered unto them.*

46

> *Rev 3:15-16 I know thy works, that thou art neither cold nor hot: I would thou wert cold or hot. So then because thou art lukewarm, and neither cold nor hot, I will spue thee out of my mouth.*

"Eternal security" is unfounded based on these Scriptures. These two words have caused people to believe that they can harbor a life-style of deliberate and premeditated sin without suffering loss. Or better yet, we can exercise, at will, our dominion over God and control His dwelling place by wrestling Scriptures to fit our traditions or the doctrine of devils that we adopt. Enough said.

The aforementioned Scriptures clearly speak of a God who is not going to be mocked (Gal. 6:7). The thrust of salvation is not found in the hope of being saved in our sin but rather, out of our sin! If we are left to this, we are found to be men most miserable. We have believed in vain. Why? For if we continue in our sin, then Christ is not risen; He still yet abides in the grave. Whenever the argument purports to benefit the flesh and directly or indirectly imply that the cross exhibited some sort of weakness, void of power to fully deliver mankind from sin, that doctrine is not only wrong but demonic. Satan attacks the Scripture with subtleties that deal with our salvation and the death, burial and resurrection of Jesus Christ as Lord and Savior.

So, let it be established that if there is no potential to lose, there is truly no potential to gain. This allows me to effectively delve into the issue of chastisement to reveal why and how it validates our salvation. It is a stamp of approval that only God gives and administrates.

47

2. Not Making Christ our Pattern of Salvation

What a delight to experience the vibrant expression of spiritual truths that bring a dynamic and universal expression of understanding that to believe in God is bliss. From the Old Testament to the very heated scene of Jesus confronting the scribes and Pharisees, we behold the divine protocol of this salvation message unfold. That message has one central theme that can be traced from the Garden of Eden until the consummation of time in Revelation. It has been God's divine purpose to procure to Himself sons out of every generation of men who would obey Him and be conformed to the image of His Son, Jesus Christ. This is why we are to look unto Jesus, for He is our standard and pattern of salvation.

> *Heb12:1,2 Wherefore seeing we also are compassed about with so great a cloud of witnesses, let us lay aside every weight, and the sin which doth so easily beset us, and let us run with patience the race that is set before us, Looking unto Jesus the author and finisher of our faith; who for the joy that was set before him endured the cross, despising the shame, and is set down at the right hand of the throne of God.*

If you ever want to know the intent of a book, a design or a covenant, it is mandatory that you have the interpretation of the author and the finisher of it. The cross that Christ endured represented the punishment of our sins upon Himself. It revealed that it was not possible for Him to be hailed "Savior" without the endurance that a savior must taste death for those that he intends to save. Further, He despised the shame that was associated with this task meaning that He was not ashamed. Then He took an eternal seat in the heavens at the right hand of the Father.

This establishes an important axiom in God's dealings with us as sons. We have a cross to endure. Not so much the trials that we face in and of themselves, but the reasons why we face them. Many times, we find ourselves in circumstances, measuring only the circumstance while failing to realize that God is using these situations for a far greater purpose; to get us to a place of obedience. He is chastising us. Chas-

48

tisement is God's method to bring us to a life-style of perpetual obedience to His voice. Without this, there is no basis of relationship and He will not take ownership of those who refuse His correction. The refusal of His correction is the refusal of His sovereign rights as Father. This is not a denial of faith, for He will remain faithful. However, it is a denial of Father. When we deny Him as our Father, our faith becomes irrelevant because it loses its objective: obedience to God the Father. It reveals that our relationship is merely with faith itself and that our loyalty is really to our own hearts.

The wilderness experience for the children of Israel was nothing more than a chastisement for not mixing the things they heard with faith. Therefore, they missed the promised land and wandered aimlessly for 40 years. However, Joshua's generation was spared because they obeyed God.

> *2 Tim 2:13 If we believe not, yet he abideth faithful: he cannot deny himself.*

There is no single, core reason why the position of a bastard occurs. It is a company of reasons. One reason stems from false doctrine, another is the rebellious nature of the heart and the rest can be summed up in the commandments and the traditions of men.

> *Mk 7:13 Making the word of God of none effect through your tradition, which ye have delivered: and many such like things do ye.*

Of a truth, the blind shall lead the blind and they both shall fall into the ditch. So let it not come as a surprise to us that many people won't ever know Him according to the truth because they were flatly deceived.

49

3. Not Willing to Endure

Heb 12:3-5 For consider him that endured such contra-diction of sinners against himself, lest ye be wearied and faint in your minds. Ye have not yet resisted unto blood, striving against sin. And ye have forgotten the exhortation which speaketh unto you as unto children, My son, despise not thou the chastening of the Lord, nor faint when thou art rebuked of him:

The reaction to chastisement is not to develop a new doctrine for that would be a false doctrine. The reason why this apostate condition has happened is because we have refused to endure His chastisement. The only way that we are able to endure it is to consider Jesus, the One who authored it. If we take our eyes off Christ, our standard, then our sole option is to become weary and faint in our minds. If this takes place, we will change our mind and draw back unto perdition and it is clear that His soul will have no pleasure in this (Heb.10:39).

Furthermore, according to Scripture, we have no excuse to become weary and faint. We have no reason to refuse His chastisement because He is faithful not to put upon us more than we can bear. We have not resisted against sin to that of blood as Christ did.

And yet, there are those who have sealed their testimony with their death because they were graced to do so.

4. Phileo Love not Agape Love

50

Heb 12:6,7 For whom the Lord loveth he chasteneth, and scourgeth every son whom he receiveth. If ye endure chastening, God dealeth with you as with sons; for what son is he whom the father chasteneth not?

Much of the present conversation occurring among Christians in this day and age is nothing more than humanistic and soulish. We have reduced the love of Christ to an idea of men. The love of God does not rejoice in iniquity. If we misinterpret His love as that of a human, we will reject His chastisement and label it legalistic. Hasn't this happened? Haven't we seen doctrines shuffled to the side because of the grand old argument that "God loves you," "He understands" and other mushy, nice sounding arguments that, when presented without balance of God's character, prevail in keeping people entrenched in their sins?

Having an eternal hope in the Son of God is radical. Placing your faith and the hope of heaven in the only religion that rejects other religions will invite persecution and direct opposition from the devil. Satan's greatest weapon within the Church today is smart men who have crept in unawares (Jude 1:4) and made the Word of God the word of men. Such remove the holy requirements of God to make it palatable for a wicked generation. We fail to realize that God is not trying to save the entire world. The world lies in wickedness and will *never* receive the Son of God (1John 5:19). He offers salvation to all who would receive it but not all will. His kingdom is not of this world (John 18:36). He did not come to bring peace, but a sword; not to join together, but to divide a mother against her daughter and a son against his father. This is a radical message and no matter how appealing we try to make it, those who are of their father the devil and have not been chosen to know Him will always reject chastisement! They want phileo love, not agape love!

5. No Correction

Heb 12:8 But if ye be without chastisement, whereof all are partakers, then are ye bastards, and not sons.

The condition of a person who refuses God's rights as Father is simply a bastard. There is no other word for it. The writer to the

Hebrews stated plainly that "if ye" not, "if they." He is talking to those who name the name of Christ. The acid test of sonship is whether or not you have been chastised. You can be baptized, you can become a member of a church, you can even speak in tongues, but if you are without correction, because you flatly refuse it, you are a bastard.

No one is excluded from this process, not even those who rush off to seminary to qualify themselves to preach this eternal Gospel. You can learn about God in a classroom for 20 years, but that doesn't mean you know Him. Greek and Hebrew is great, but it doesn't excuse anyone from going through His schooling; chastisement. I appreciate the knowledge that is available in our theological settings, but knowledge alone will guarantee error. No living human being can call themselves to the ministry for it is a call of God. Whom God calls, God qualifies.

Heb 5:4,5 And no man taketh this honour unto himself, but he that is called of God, as was Aaron. In the same way, Christ glorified not Himself to be made High Priest; but He that said unto him, thou art my Son, to day have I begotten thee.

Heb 1:5 For unto which of the angels said he at any time, Thou art my Son, this day have I begotten thee? And again, I will be to him a Father, and he shall be to me a Son?

It was God who called His Son forth and it was God who made Him High Priest. The core reason why we have such a lack of repentance in this nation is because we have a lack of strong men in the pulpit who have been chastised to the degree that they are free from men. This is one of the main reasons why we have bastards in the pulpit. They have not been made by God. They are without chastisement and therefore, without God's Spirit upon them to bear witness to the truth and to declare a word that would break up hardened hearts that the word of God may be sown.

I perceive it necessary for me to simply state that I understand the words that I am using to illustrate this point appear to be without compassion and understanding. Perhaps these words are not for you to hear. Don't misinterpret this to be a message of condemnation. This message is designed to address some grievances that God has with His people especially, His leaders. It is designed to provoke and ignite a holy passion for God's people to return to Him with all of their heart and realize that God will not wink at our rebellion but instead, will provide a warning for us to return and repent.

6. Partakers of His Holiness

Heb 12:9,10 Furthermore we have had fathers of our flesh which corrected us, and we gave them reverence: shall we not much rather be in subjection unto the Father of spirits, and live? For they verily for a few days chastened us after their own pleasure; but he for our profit, that we might be partakers of his holiness.

We understand the correction that our natural fathers meted out to us and why they did: to make us better people. For this, we respect them and give them reverence. Why is it that we have come to believe that God's rights as Father are less? His reasons far extend simply wanting to make us better; He wants to make us *holy.* Chastisement is God's way of developing His likeness in us. It is the process of removing that which offends and establishing that which honors. He is making us into vessels of His holy nature that are met for His use. Striving is one thing, but striving lawfully is all that matters.

53

> *2 Tim 2:20,21 But in a great house there are not only vessels of gold and of silver, but also of wood and of earth; and some to honour, and some to dishonour. If a man therefore purge himself from these, he shall be a vessel unto honour, sanctified, and meet for the master's use, and prepared unto every good work.*

When we give ourselves to understand that salvation has to do with God, it sounds simple and would appear to be a redundant statement. However, the business of religion today doesn't always see it that way. There are countless counterfeits that are prepared to cast you into prison if you questioned their beliefs. I am speaking directly about those who name the name of Christ. There are men who have made themselves apostles for the business of religion, not for the business of God.

> *2 Cor 11:13-15 For such are false apostles, deceitful workers, transforming themselves into the apostles of Christ. And no marvel; for Satan himself is transformed into an angel of light. Therefore it is no great thing if his ministers also be transformed as the ministers of righteousness; whose end shall be according to their works.*

Paul calls them his (satan's) ministers. What is the evidence of who their father is? No chastisement. They are bastards who have no heart and will flatter you to the bank every Sunday. The reasons why this word is perhaps shocking is because it's not being declared. It's not positive. It's not American. Well, God is not an American; He is God. The nations are but a drop in the bucket and they that forget God shall perish.

54

> *Job 8:12,13 Whilst it is yet in his greenness, and not cut down, it withereth before any other herb. So are the paths of all that forget God; and the hypocrite's hope shall perish:*

Psa 9:17 The wicked shall be turned into hell, and all the nations that forget God.

As we behold world events unfold before our eyes and witness our country move into a time of transition of war and economic change, we must be aware that God is in total control. He allows and disallows. There is nothing that happens on the stage of mankind without His permission. Even as generations before faced tragic and catastrophic loss, so will we face it in this generation. As we beheld the horrible events of 9/11, we would do well to always live in a state of readiness of God's purposes unfolding upon the earth. Wars are allowed for purposes that we are not aware of. Jesus stated there would be wars and rumors of wars and that does not exclude America, Christians in America, or American Christians.

I say this because those who have endured chastisement have no interest but God's at heart. This is why we need not be dismayed when we see what He forewarned us come to pass. We need not be discouraged. It is not that we are happy when events like this happen because we grieve and mourn also. Nonetheless, we have a peace that surpasses understanding for He has promised to keep us in perfect peace as we keep our minds stayed on Him.

Ever wonder why there is not much preaching about Jesus' soon return? Why is there not a clarion call to prepare ourselves for His righteous judgment? It's not a comfortable thought, that's why. Let it be understood that there are men and women of God who are preaching a powerful word today. They are not compromising. They are hearing the voice of the Lord and are not holding back. They are pressing and encouraging others to press. They are enduring chastisement and you can see the fruit coming forth. And I realize that no matter how much you preach the truth and how many signs and wonders go forth, it is still possible for the heart to harden against God. All we can do as those who declare the truth with power is to be faithful to deliver God's Word and trust Him to watch over it. It's not a personal issue between *God's people* and me; it's personal between *God* and me! Yes, I fellowship, but not after the flesh, nor will I subject myself to men. When I say "subject", I do not mean under leadership - I mean it to be as I would subject myself to Christ Himself. You might think this to be obvious, but there are countless people who assume that the word of their pastor or bishop is a word that does not need to be qualified by the Word of God. That's not scriptural! All men are subject to error even in their most sincere undertakings. Follow men as they follow Christ.

7. We Don't Believe in the Necessity of Fruit

> *Heb 12:11 Now no chastening for the present seemeth to be joyous, but grievous: nevertheless afterward it yieldeth the peaceable fruit of righteousness unto them which are exercised thereby.*

I summarize this section on the realization that articulating the scriptural requirement for bringing forth fruit met with repentance is scarce and, in some circles, not even preached or taught. Though I am not at every church on Sunday listening to every preacher preach, I discern by the climate of this age and the standard amongst the notable leaders of this generation, a forsaking of the tenets of the faith that separates us from sinners and make us a holy nation. The tenets of our faith truly make us a "called out" people.

Let's just be frank and understand that the agenda of today has more to do with the pride of men, the size of churches and the political aspirations of ambitious individuals. I'll be a marked man for saying it. But I've been chastised and continue to endure it so I'm a dead man walking and realize that no man can stay the hand of God upon a man whether it be me or another individual. God is going to get His message heard and He will use death to remove someone if He has to. He's done so from the beginning of time because life and death rest with Him.

Though the chastisement of God is not enjoyable but painful, nevertheless, when it has completed its work, fruit comes forth upon those who have been exercised by it. Upon those who embrace this process, there shall come forth fruit. He will purge us even more to bring forth more fruit (John 15:2b).

There is a world coming: a new heaven and a new earth. There will be no more tears. No more pain. No more death. We shall reign with Him throughout eternity. He shall be with us and talk with us and He will be unto us a Father and we shall be unto Him sons of righteousness who shall rule in the heavens. Even now, we sit with Him by faith in heavenly places carrying forth the Word of righteousness to a dying world. That word comes forth from vessels who have been conformed to it themselves. Let us fear, lest after we ourselves have preached to others, we become castaways (1Cor. 9:27).

Be encouraged and know that the chastisement we endure fulfills His word. For was not the chastisement of our peace upon Him? Had He not endured this chastisement, Christ Himself would not be a Son and therefore, not worthy to be made High Priest to offer sacrifices for those who seek salvation. Furthermore, salvation would not be sought unless God drew us to Himself. It would do us well to remember that we have not chosen Him but He has chosen us that we should bring forth fruit to His name. But praise God - He is our High Priest and therefore, assures us that we also can endure for what He endured, He endured as a man, yet being God.

57

THE NATIONS

Our nations are quickly yielding to the spirit of Antichrist as prophesied through God's word. America, with its thousands upon thousands of churches, produces only tens upon tens of fruit. As a nation, it has more vehemently than ever rejected the idea of God as its Father, and yet we insist that this is a Christian nation. We rage battle against White House politics and picket abortion clinics in response to the murders of innocent children. Through human philosophies, we want to believe that we wrestle against flesh and blood. Our efforts to bring the Gospel to the lost are being met with results that are questionable. Certainly, there are times to demonstrate righteousness by taking a public stand, however, we must be led of God solely in every action that we undertake for His Kingdom.

Salvation has come to mean so many things that very few understand what they have done by accepting Jesus Christ as Lord of their lives. Thousands receive the idea that Christ has forgiven them of their sins, but cannot keep them from their sins. Why is this being taught? Because you cannot make a bastard into a son! It is to do away with the chastisement and scourging that God places upon everyone whom He has chosen (Hebrews 12:6). It is to preach a Gospel without the standard of sonship and therefore, a Gospel that is without consequences. What need is it to work out our salvation in fear and trembling if we stand not to lose the things that we have so labored for (2 Jo 1:8)? Have we believed in vain (1 Co 15:2)? Shall we be as a pig and return to our mud, or a dog and eat our vomit (2 Pet 2:22)? How shall God judge the world if such ideas be true?

> *Ro 3:5,6 But if our unrighteousness commend the righteousness of God, what shall we say? [Is] God unrighteous who*

taketh vengeance? (I speak as a man) God forbid: for then how shall God judge the world?

This is what is tainting Christianity - a mixture of ideas and religions that provide excuses to be without chastisement. In other words, we simply desire our way, but want the privileges of sons of God as well.

We insist that God save the nation in which we live, but fail to realize that *we* are a nation - A HOLY NATION!

1Pet 2:9 But ye are a chosen generation, a royal priesthood, an holy nation, a peculiar people; that ye should shew forth the praises of him who hath called you out of darkness into his marvellous light:

There are many issues in our country to take a stand for, however, we must seek the issue of God's kingdom, not the kingdoms of the world. Yes, we must declare abortion as a sin before God, only after we have declared His righteousness through our obedience, which is a result of His chastisement.

Even at the expense of innocent lives, we must not forget that the issues of this life should not replace the issues of God's will; to learn to obey His voice and produce the fruit of righteousness that He might not be ashamed to call us sons.

The nation of America says, "In God We Trust", yet it is not the God of the Holy Bible. It is one of their own making, for if God were their Father, they would love Jesus.

John 8:42 Jesus said unto them, If God were your Father, ye would love me: for I proceeded forth and came from God; neither came I of myself, but he sent me.

59

It is imperative that our thinking about any nation remain in the context of God's word and not borderline on humanistic traditions. Just because it sounds nice does not make it right. Thus, "God save America" sounds nice, but it is not right. God is not going to save any nation - He is calling a people *out* of every nation to form His holy nation! These are the dangers of "positive thinking." Such philosophies are dangerous and are causing many mainstream Christian leaders to entertain the children of the world. "Positive thinking" gurus are accepted as those who have good news or can provide "motivation" for God's people. God does not motivate - He inspires!

OUR HOMES

This issue centers on the lack of fathers and because of that, America could be labeled a land of bastards. Everywhere you look, there is an illegitimate child or one that is not being disciplined. Children are as rebellious as ever, and marriages are with men but without husbands and fathers. The condition in our nation stands as a witness against our pulpits. Judgment must first originate at the house of God. Men are running away from the realities of fatherhood, either physically or mentally. For the sake of "peace" we overlook discipline. This does not make peace—it makes bastards! Instead of loving our wives with the power of God's truth, we hate them with humanistic philosophies. Our homes have failed at the idea of America's dream including that of Dr. Martin Luther King's dream. Whites and Blacks living together on earth is certainly an effort and idea that is commendable by men, but if the righteousness of God and obedience to His voice is not your dream, you are headed for a nightmare. His mandate was not to bring racial reconciliation. Jesus' mandate was to reconcile man back to God, not to each other. Therefore, He came to divide everyone for the sake of His Father.

We have looked to men to father our families rather than God, and therefore, we depend on systems, organizations and democratic rules to make our families strong, our marriages thriving, and our children healthy. Yet, we will not allow God to father us, nurture us and teach us His ways and His nature. We believed His holiness to be impossible and totally unrealistic, and thus, our homes have become battlegrounds on which husband beats wife, and wife beats child. We have nurtured an institution of chaos whereby our children are fed a rebellious diet watching rebellious violence on television while wearing rebellious clothing.

You would not believe it but these same families attend church, shake the pastor's hand every week, and yet expect nothing from the church to solve their dilemma. How can they when the pastor's son comes over to play demonic games with their son each week? Bastards in the pulpit are the cause of bastards in our homes!

Our daughters are lost in the dilemma of sexuality, unable to exercise constraint over themselves in apparel as well as in desire. In the depths of their being, they desire to be a woman of God, holy and pure, and yet it seems a far distant dream. Their fathers have not instructed them. Their own brothers do not respect them. Unfortunately, it is not uncommon for Pastor's daughters to have a baby shower with no husband for them and no father for the child.

It is the preacher who instills the voice of God in a nation, in a community and in the homes. But, they are turned out of the way. They have refused the fire of God's purging and have chosen the path of ease and the ways of the flesh. They have, in essence, yielded to the ideas of men and the temptation of pride.

Isa 56:10–11 His watchmen are blind: they are all igno-rant, they are all dumb dogs, they cannot bark; sleeping, lying down, loving to slumber. Yea, they are greedy dogs which can never have enough, and they are shepherds that cannot un-derstand: they all look to their own way, every one for his gain, from his quarter.

John 15:2 Every branch in me that beareth not fruit he taketh away: and every branch that beareth fruit, he purgeth it, that it may bring forth more fruit.

When God's due order is truly accepted, every man will become the head of his own home. He will be the pastor of his wife and shep-herd her. He will be the voice that his children hearken to and obey.

Our homes have yielded to the traditions of men and have made the word of God of no effect. Many men in the Body of Christ send their families off to church to hear the word of God from another man, while having no desire or intention for their wives and children to hear God's word from their own lips. As pastors, we have irrespon-sibly allowed the headships of our homes to shift their duties onto us and have said little or nothing to reveal that they must wash their own wives with the water of the word. They must train their own children to become obedient and controllable.

The truth of a fellowship is not evident in the mere doctrine of the Bible. It is not enough for us to teach truth. It will do us no good if we merely sing our praises to God with fleshly emotions and self–motivated concepts labeled "revelation." The devil recognizes that al-though we possess all the religious forms and formulas, without a con-frontation of sin and rebellion in our families, our wives, husbands, and children, we will fail to bring change! We have denied the faith!

One might say, "Mr. Owens, you are being too critical and your words lack compassion." Such fleshly, humanistic statements reveal why the Gospel is powerless in one's life. It reveals that one has not truly accepted the rule and leadership of the Lord Jesus Christ. Instead, such a person has chosen to have respect unto themselves and others.

True compassion will drive thieves out of God's temple.

Jude 1:16 These are murmurers, complainers, walking after their own lusts; and their mouth speaketh great swelling words, having men's persons in admiration because of advantage.

I am motivated by God's love, not man's love. My words are heavy because we do not have time to play games and to discuss issues. It is time for God to be God, or for baal to be god. It is time for Christians to stop baking cakes for their idols and return to the One and True God of the Holy Bible and worship Him only.

1Kings 18:21 And Elijah came unto all the people, and said, How long halt ye between two opinions? if the LORD be God, follow him: but if Baal, then follow him. And the people answered him not a word.

We have ranted and raved about judgment coming upon the Church and when it comes, we are speechless and unable to stand against the tide of rejection. As a result, we make excuses. The excuses we use are really good ones. They are political, religious and have much sound reasoning to support them. But, they are powerless in bringing change within the heart of man. God will release His fury upon the rebellious and those who have refused His correction after the voice of His prophets rise up and give warning. It is written:

> *Amos 3:6–8 Shall a trumpet be blown in the city, and the people not be afraid? shall there be evil in a city, and the LORD hath not done it? Surely the Lord GOD will do nothing, but he revealeth his secret unto his servants the prophets. The lion hath roared, who will not fear? the Lord GOD hath spoken, who can but prophesy?*

Can we be real and accept the fact that Church is big business today and members are shifting from one church to another? Why? Because they have no sanctuary at home. The local assembly will never replace home sanctuary. God never designed the public gathering of His people to be controlled by one man, one gift, or one voice, but instead, by the many gifts of the Spirit whereby families can be perfected, instructed and joined together. The public gathering is where families who have home sanctuary come together to give to and receive from other families what they have received from God through the husband at home.

HUSBANDS AND WIVES

Chapters 5 and 6 of Ephesians do not indicate anything regarding the local assembly being involved with the order of the home. Ephesians chapter 4 does not suggest that the fivefold ministry is involved with the order of the home in a direct and tangible way. These gifts are to be used within the Body of Christ in the local assembly. We have confused the local assembly with our home. The greatest house in the world is not the White House; it is your House! When you leave church, you go home. When you leave your job, you go home. When you leave the stores, you go home. Home is where you experience the reality of life. Men, no one can build your home except you. God's order is clear.

64

Observe what Chapter 5 reveals:

v.22 Wives, submit to your husbands.

v.25 Husbands, love your wives.

v.26 (husbands) Sanctify and cleanse her with the washing of the water by the word.

v.27 That he (Christ/husband) might present it to himself a glorious church (wife).

Observe what Chapter 6 reveals:

v. 1 Children obey your parents (before others) in the Lord.

v. 2 Honor thy father and mother (then church leadership).

v. 3 Fathers provoke not your children.

Though we are to honor our leadership, the point is our parents and our family come first. As well, the first epistle of Corinthians direct the wife to seek instruction from her husband at home.

> *1Cor 14:34, 35 Let your women keep silence in the churches: for it is not permitted unto them to speak; but they are commanded to be under obedience. And if they will learn any thing, let them ask their husbands at home: for it is a shame for women to speak in the church.*

It clearly states that if wives will learn anything, let them ask their husbands at home. How powerful this word is to our pastors across this nation. When we fail to admonish our men to teach the word of God at home, we have failed to give them the whole counsel of God. In essence, we want to possess all the knowledge and keep others from understanding, lest they become the men of God, husbands and fathers that they are! We believe it threatens our vision and the support of it.

The Body of Christ receives its edification as a body assembly.

> *Eph 4:11, 12 And he gave some, apostles; and some, prophets; and some, evangelists; and some, pastors and teachers; For the perfecting of the saints, for the work of the ministry, for the edifying of the body of Christ:*

It is certain that everything we receive from our local assembly is for every area of our life, nonetheless, the application of it can only be applied and made a reality in the home.

HUSBANDS

The role of the man has been belittled, despised and attacked by men and women alike, but we must understand that satan is the mastermind behind this diabolical scheme to pervert, confuse and totally arrest the authority figure in our nation and homes.

Husbands have been ideally categorized as the breadwinner, the lawn mower boy, the fixer upper and the wife–pleaser both sexually and socially. Sadly, he is viewed as a convenience, not a conqueror, a trophy to brag to others about. He is a toy that tickles on demand and when exhausted, he is the sofa bum, the remote control expert and the soda or beer guzzler.

In today's society, the husband has become everything except the image of God to our wives and children, our communities and our nation. The result of unchastised pastors and those in the vineyard of God's heritage have produced a generation of men essentially void of godly fervor or temperance. The majority of husbands are spiritually (and physically) unfit and therefore, unable or unwilling to stand for

66

righteousness with their peers. Compliance with the majority is the norm. By taking a stand for righteousness against the deceived majority, one is branded as out of order, rebellious and/or super spiritual.

The true acid test of an effective leader is not how large an offering he can take. It is not how well he gets along with his community leaders. It is not demonstrated in how he shakes everyone's hand after church in an effort to reflect good social skills. His humorous, shallow jokes that are intended to flatter matters not. Nor is it his "M. Div.", "Dr." status, or denominational ordination combined with his secured 300 plus members and $3,000.00 per month income that renders him effective. An effective leader is not one due to the social and religious traditional standards that have crept in and become the norm.

The true acid test of a God fearing, effective, bonafide pastor is that he produces conscience stricken, holy living, Scripture quoting men of God!

> *Job 38:3 Gird up now thy loins like a man; for I will demand of thee, and answer thou me.*

If our pulpits are void of men chastened of God, so will our pews be. I am not talking about the standards of the world that many churches emphasize with much zeal such as paying your bills on time, earning good money, keeping your lawn neat and attending Sunday school. Such shallow standards produce the kind of "men" that many pastors want. Such are not characterized by the standard of God's word as men. While these standards have value and are important, they become idols when equated with the higher commandments that Christ left us. Jesus warned leaders about this mindset. He declared:

> *Mt 23:23 Woe unto you, scribes and Pharisees, hypocrites! for ye pay tithe of mint and anise and cummin, and*

67

have omitted the weightier [matters] of the law, judgment, mercy, and faith: these ought ye to have done, and not to leave the other undone.

- David ran for his life and lived in caves, but he obeyed God.

- Job refused to curse God as his wife suggested and was restored twice what satan had stolen.

- Elijah, full of faith and brazen in appearance, ate from a widow's table, yet he stopped rain and dew for 3 years.

- Paul considered everything as dung, including his education, birthright and countrymen in order to know Christ and the power of His resurrection.

While it is imperative that we provide the necessities of life for our families, our passion should aim to provide the eternal necessities first and foremost. Today's husbands have set their gaze upon this world, which is passing away in its present form, rather than on eternal life that yields eternal dividends.

2 Cor 4:18 While we look not at the things which are seen, but at the things which are not seen: for the things which are seen are temporal; but the things which are not seen are eternal.

The husband who names the name of Christ must do so with godly fear, understanding that his position toward his wife is compared to that of Christ loving the Church. Therefore, he must prepare

68 for a judgment that reflects this level of responsibility.

The seriousness of loving our wives in the sight of God is paramount seeing that if we do not honor them and understand their needs, our prayers will be hindered.

> *1 Pet 3:7 Likewise, ye husbands, dwell with them according to knowledge, giving honour unto the wife, as unto the weaker vessel, and as being heirs together of the grace of life; that your prayers be not hindered.*

When we reflect upon the scandals that have brought a reproach upon the name of Christ, most have been of a sexual nature. Imagine the hundreds of thousands of sexually related agendas that exist in the Church today that are hidden or ignored altogether. Simply observe the manner in which women order themselves and how men are more concerned with their outward appeal than the inward condition of the heart.

American Christianity has become a high fashion, soulish religion that reflects passion for self rather than love for a Savior. Yes, church members call upon the name of Yahweh but with glossed, cherry painted lips and teenagers harboring a life-style that is contrary to Christian profession. Men lift up hands to show how much they love the Lord, yet their eyes are lifting up dresses all the while. The Church has lost its purpose when appearance is the primary issue rather than who we really are.

Bear with me. I understand that those listed above are human and that no church setting is perfect. I am perfectly aware that we are working out our salvation in fear and trembling, yet when you take a true assessment of the situation, many are choosing to make provision for the flesh when Christ has made provision for us to crucify it!

> *Rom 6:10–12 For in that he died, he died unto sin once: but in that he liveth, he liveth unto God. Likewise reckon ye also yourselves to be dead indeed unto sin, but alive unto God through Jesus Christ our Lord. Let not sin therefore reign in your mortal body, that ye should obey it in the lusts thereof.*

We continue to rebel when we attempt to make sin appear not to be sin. When we acquaint ourselves with friends of the world whose affections and aspirations are after this life, we are attempting to re-write God's Word and alter His standard.

The issues that plague our churches are numerous, and many of our leaders are ignoring this truth. Perhaps it is due to denial of God's protocol in bringing our actions to accountability. Perhaps we are simply weak in our minds and fear the people and thus, say nothing.

Initially, it stems from the fact that we are not producing godly homes. Instead, we are producing memberships. Our focus as pastors must return to Christ alone—the foundation on which God builds His Church. Jesus Christ is the Chief Cornerstone. There is no other foundation on which we can build. As the man or woman builds their life upon Christ, Christ will build His Church within their hearts. Let me clearly state that there are great works going forth in our country. Despite our leadership crises, God is yet managing His people.

There are churches that are responsible for changing whole cities. Many men across this nation would have died or remained without the hope of Christ in their lives had community churches not stood in the gap. However, there is a leaven in our midst and God will not overlook it because of our deeds.

Husband, be careful if you are naming the name of Christ. God will inspect your wife and you will be held accountable for her attire. She may have the finest clothes and the most polished shoes. Her hair can be as smooth as silk, and her jewelry of the finest quality. Her associates can be of the "upper church" class, and she may have servants at her disposal. She sits on the podium before thousands as you dance and shout down the glory of the Lord. You even brag about how wonderful she is, and she returns your boast with a religious smile.

Yet when it is all said and done and God's testing fire is unleashed upon her, will hair remain upon her head, or will there be a burnt scalp? Will she be clothed or naked? Will her relationships prove genuine, or will she be found in the company of gossipers and backbiters? Will her odor be turned from Chanel to a stench, or will she maintain a sweet smelling savor to the nostrils of God?

The husband has one standard that he must uphold before his wife and it is not to be confused with the world's view, her tendencies, or even your own opinion. It is clearly defined in God's word.

> *1 Pet 3:3,4 Whose adorning let it not be that outward adorning of plaiting the hair, and of wearing of gold, or of putting on of apparel; But let it be the hidden man of the heart, in that which is not corruptible, even the ornament of a meek and quiet spirit, which is in the sight of God of great price.*

A WORD OF INSTRUCTION

I admonish the husbands who are reading this book to gird up the loins of your mind and take godly control of your wife for God's sake, not your own. Do so for God's glory, not hers. This must first happen in the secret place of prayer. Repent before God for any negligence on your part. Repentance takes time. You must feel the wrong and allow it to work godly sorrow. This way, true repentance will occur and corresponding action will follow.

2 Cor 7:9–12 Now I rejoice, not that ye were made sorry, but that ye sorrowed to repentance: for ye were made sorry after a godly manner, that ye might receive damage by us in nothing. For godly sorrow worketh repentance to salvation not to be repented of: but the sorrow of the world worketh death. For behold this selfsame thing, that ye sorrowed after a godly sort, what carefulness it wrought in you, yea, what clearing of yourselves, yea, what indignation, yea, what fear, yea, what vehement desire, yea, what zeal, yea, what revenge! In all things ye have approved yourselves to be clear in this matter. Wherefore, though I wrote unto you, I did it not for his cause that had done the wrong, nor for his cause that suffered wrong, but that our care for you in the sight of God might appear unto you.

Next, you must confess your fault to her and ask for forgiveness. It is important to renew your mind and spirit with God's Word before approaching her in order to provide clear answers based on sound doctrine.

Your wife might not know quite how to handle your act of repentance. She may be pleased that you are going to assume your position as headship and pastor of your home, or she might close up at your spiritual adjustment. In either case, move in grace, faith, authority and love. Be resolute and God will honor your stand. Thus, your repentance would prove to have been a true and godly act.

Stay on track, and progress by spending time before God on a daily basis. I stress quality time, not a 15-minute donut break "prayer session." If you cannot give God at least a few hours daily - one to study and one to listen and be still, you are either working too much or playing too much. Align your priorities correctly. Change does not happen because you think it will. It happens because you act.

Once you have been forgiven, the next morning is the dawn of new beginnings in your life. If you have children, line them up from the oldest to the youngest and, with your wife by your side, conduct Bible study. Let your children stand up while you teach the family God's word for 15–30 minutes. It allows them to be more attentive. This should be done in the morning before breakfast. If you work, let your wife pray for the children before they go to school and conduct the Bible study at night or whenever the best time allows it. My family and I have church! We sing, shout, and pray as the Spirit directs our hearts. This is the most crucial part of the day. The family that will prevail in the last days will have dedicated prayer and worship habits.

This word of instruction is to provoke you to simply develop a daily plan of action to prepare your wife and children for God's judgment. God will honor those who honor Him, and shame those who reject His counsel. Remove the idols from your home that would hinder the worship of God or cause you to draw back. It will not be easy for some whose children are set in their ways. Only as you sincerely communicate God's protocol will they yield and accept. Even if they do not accept it, they will know you are standing for God and will respect you for it. God will do the rest.

To the wife, I simply encourage you to allow your husband to be God's husband to you. In this, you will experience an honor and respect that is divine. God will love you through him, but you must submit and allow it to come forth. Remember, your husband is still flesh and blood, so be patient and God will bring it to pass.

Blessed be the Lord, for God is raising up husbands who will arise and say along with Joshua:

73

> *Josh 24:14 Now therefore fear the LORD, and serve him in sincerity and in truth: and put away the gods which your fathers served on the other side of the flood, and in Egypt; and serve ye the LORD.*

The greatest impact any one person has upon the home will be found in the role of the father. Our homes, churches, and nation must face this issue squarely with grace and endeavor to understand God's protocol in this area of tremendous influence upon the lives of every living soul.

 # FATHERS OF OUR HOMES

*Pro 17:6 Children's children are the crown of old men;
and the glory of children are their fathers.*

This is the question that you and I must answer. They might have every carnal convenience at their disposal, but do your children possess glory?

The children of this world should expect rebellion and chaos in the home because they are without God. But the children of God have adopted a wicked norm that leaves our children without the radiance of God upon them. When the father is fathering, there will be a glory about them and that glory will reflect him. The church nursery and children's church cannot accomplish this.

When my children were young and accompanied my wife and I to events or restaurants, we would always receive praise from people regarding their public conduct. This was the result of how we reared them in the private confines of our home.

Years ago when they were much younger, we attended a church service which was over 2 hours long (and that was just the preaching). True to form, they sat there without one complaint. The people were so amazed that they kept looking at them as much as the preacher! Praise God!

After service, several people approached my wife and I and specifically addressed me concerning our children on how well trained they are, but they addressed my wife on how sweet they are. I am told that I have a blessed family and they understand that I have built this family upon the foundation of the Lord. They tell my wife that she has a blessed family and their voice indicates that they understand that she has submitted to the leadership of her husband and allowed the rearing of our children to take place.

You see, it is the father that is the glory of the children, and the wife reveals the true character of her husband when and if that husband is in the Lord. When I say, "reveal the true character", it is not that I am implying they are without their own character. I speak this in respect to the mystery of Christ and His bride. When the marriage is operating in respect to God's intention for marriage, our wives are likened to the Body of Christ and as the Body of Christ, we reveal Christ to the world through our lives and conduct. So likewise, our wives reveal the true character, or the lack thereof, in their husbands. Now understand, though the wife's character is impeccable, honorable and truly reveals Christ, if her husband is void of these godly characteristics, she will yet reveal it for they are one. Because she carries his name, she reveals this. This revealing it is not a reproach upon her, but on him. This is why if a man desires the office of a bishop, his wife must be an example of his character. Otherwise, he is not fit to lead God's people.

The temperament of the majority of local churches concerning children will reflect the temperament of the pastor's own children. If they are not fathered with a strong arm of love and trained with a standard being declared from the pulpit, then neither will the fathers in that church demand it of their seed.

Bastards in the pulpit are men who have rejected the chastening of God their Father. They have said, "no" to His purging and His way, and have made excuses for not pressing beyond their present state. The reason for God's chastisement is that we may be partakers of His holiness in order to yield the peaceable fruit of righteousness.

> *Heb 12:10, 11 For they verily for a few days chastened us after their own pleasure; but he for our profit, that we might be partakers of his holiness. Now no chastening for the present seemeth to be joyous, but grievous: nevertheless afterward it yieldeth the peaceable fruit of righteousness unto them which are exercised thereby.*

If those in the pulpit are without chastisement, likewise, so will the sons of that church be. There are those fathers, however, who see this and have not allowed that spirit to transfer to their lives or to their sons. As they continue to press into God's fullness, they will outgrow that leadership. I will expound on this further in the section entitled, "Fathers of Our Churches."

It is unfortunate that families are divided during church service. Most children are so undisciplined that they have to be sent to children's church. Sugar ladened punch, cookies, videos and an occasional Bible study are the norm. Entertainment, in an effort to control, is the preferred method to attempt to handle children who have not been trained in the ways of God.

> *Pro 22:6 Train up a child in the way he should go: and when he is old, he will not depart from it.*

As fathers, we are to "train up" our children. The word "train" denotes a most definite learning. We interpret it to mean saying "no" four or five times or to discuss the issue with our children for their approval. We play mind games and make promises to gain their cooperation. This is definitely training—the child is training the parent!

The word "train" in the Hebrew is "chanak." It means "to imitate or discipline or to dedicate." This signifies the idea of a clear, concise objective in the mind of the trainer. There is a specific way in which he has determined his child will go. There are no gray areas or opinions about it, and as a result, he is resolute to train his seed "in the way he should go", not in the way that he wants to go, or even the way you or others want him to go.

That "way" varies from child to child. We must train them based on the way that God has made them. We must not misinterpret this to mean for us to determine what our child will be in life, but instead, cause our children to become aware of who they are and what God has purposed them to be. It is this objective that we are to have in mind when we are training them for the glory of God.

Every mother "feels" in her heart what is right. There is a saying in the world, which claims that since your own mother wiped your rear and can still smell milk on your breath, she supposedly knows what is best for your child. Everyone wants his or her approach to be the way your child should go but you must discern the correct approach, which is revealed by having a relevant relationship with God through His Son, Jesus Christ.

These are some of the traditional stories that have produced an array of results within the baby boomer generation. We are also starting to experience serious problems among our youth ranging from sexual immorality that encompasses homosexuality, fornication and adultery. I believe when parents fail to establish correction through allowing consequences to be experienced by our children, it will manifest in their lives in various forms. I am not suggesting that it is limited only to sexual problems, however, as we see the ever increasing rate of abuse in this area, we cannot ignore the fact that passions left unrestrained and unchecked can and will produce a generation of evil doers and sexual problems in the lives of our youth.

From this, our generation will also produce doubters rather than heroes of the faith, wimps instead of warriors, and cowards, not conquerors. The father's role is to train up the child while the mother reinforces it. Those mothers who are without a husband can still allow a man of God to become a father figure for their children by laying down the rules with authority. The mother will then reiterate the rules when necessary. We need fathers to produce fathers.

Fathers, you must understand that your sons and daughters are more important to God than your job, ministry or vision. In fact, any true ministry or vision from God will include not just you, but especially, your seed and their seed. God is after generations. God was not interested in Abraham for Abraham's sake alone. He was interested in Abraham for Christ. He needed a man who would think about others after he was gone, and not just about himself while on earth.

The very reason that God could reveal secrets to Abraham was because He knew Abraham would rear his children in obedience to His decrees and not withhold his only son from Him.

Gen 18:17–19 And the LORD said, Shall I hide from Abraham that thing which I do; Seeing that Abraham shall surely become a great and mighty nation, and all the nations

79

of the earth shall be blessed in him? For I know him, that he will command his children and his household after him, and they shall keep the way of the LORD, to do justice and judgment; that the LORD may bring upon Abraham that which he hath spoken of him.

God knows what we will do with His children by what we do with ours. As fathers, we must not confuse or mix the standards of this world with the standards of God's kingdom. If one who has denied the faith, by not providing food and shelter, is worse than an infidel, tell me then, what is the state of a believer who does not provide the things of God to his family?

In order for God to obtain the fullness of His will from you, you must transfer yourself into your children that they may continue to express God's glory in the earth because it is not possible for your lifetime to fulfill what God fully intends to accomplish. God is into legacy.

Your training is a statement of fact to God and to the devil. It proceeds past mere words. Your confession places you in a position to act, for it is faith without *works* that is dead, not faith without *words*. When fathers focus on their children and view them as God does, they will behold an eternal soul whose destination depends on their direction.

It's a sad fate to witness generation after generation come out of the Church full of religious formulas. Their fruit clearly reveals them to be "without father." They have little or no regard for authority, and the value of life has been diminished to chance and not to absolutes. They have "seen" what their fathers believe, and realize that it does not correspond to what their fathers have said. They had service at a local building, but never had church at home. They heard a preacher get excited over a passage out of Luke, but never witnessed Dad teach out of Proverbs.

In today's landscape of Christendom, the Body of Christ has not honored and valued the fathers of our homes because they have not honored the FATHER'S house.

> *John 2:16 And said unto them that sold doves, Take these things hence; make not my Father's house an house of merchandise.*

If leadership in the church desires to witness revival upon the families of their congregations, attention must be given to the area of fatherhood.

> *1 Tim 3:4 One that ruleth well his own house, having his children in subjection with all gravity;*

> *1 Tim 3:12 Let the deacons be the husbands of one wife, ruling their children and their own houses well.*

A WORD OF INSTRUCTION

> *Isa 28:9 Whom shall he teach knowledge? and whom shall he make to understand doctrine? them that are weaned from the milk, and drawn from the breasts.*

The word of the Lord to fathers is to understand when it is time to teach knowledge and to make doctrine understood. From the time that your child is weaned from milk, it is time to prepare that child for sonship.

We have coined a phrase that is far from God's truth. "He is just a baby, let him alone. He will grow out of it." Then every couple of years, it changes from being a baby to a toddler, to a little boy, to a

81

young boy, to a teenager and finally, on to a young man who never "grew out of it." This form of philosophy has been delivered to our children from one stage of rebellion to the next. It is a humanistic cover–up for a father to ignore the truth of his responsibility which is to rear his child for God's purpose.

> *Col 2:8 Beware lest any man spoil you through philosophy and vain deceit, after the tradition of men, after the rudiments of the world, and not after Christ.*

The Bible reveals that the true way to know if a father loves his child is if he disciplines that child. All other forms of expressions outside of discipline do not reflect God's protocol and therefore, rest in the ordinances and philosophies of the world.

> *Pro 13:24 He that spareth his rod hateth his son: but he that loveth him chasteneth him betimes.*

Once, while sharing with my son Ryan, I said to him, "Ryan, I am not your buddy. I am your father. I am not raising you for me. I am raising you for God." As fathers, this has to constantly be our view lest we forget that our children are given to us by God for God. When we try to turn it around for our purpose, we experience rebellious children who despise their parents for not giving them the truth coupled with correction while they were young.

> *Pro 19:18 Chasten thy son while there is hope, and let not thy soul spare for his crying.*

82

We have produced a generation of bastards who are full of anger and resentment toward authority. They were not born that way-they acquired it. We left them to themselves because we wanted to be left to ourselves.

Pro 29:15 The rod and reproof give wisdom: but a child left to himself bringeth his mother to shame.

We believe that talking and going to McDonald's gives wisdom but it does not. Only the rod of correction fostered in love and communication of what is wrong will impart the wisdom of God.

I speak to the fathers to no longer ignore the condition of their children. They either have the character of God, or they do not. They will be able to stand against the onslaught of their generation, or they will be unable to resist it. Arise to your responsibility and repent before God. With a resolved mind and resolute spirit, communicate to your children that you have made some serious mistakes. Identify them and apologize.

It is important that you inform them that there will be changes in the home and that it will not be easy. Make this emphatically clear. It would be wise to detail the changes and explain the benefits that accompany them. Immediately encourage your family that, through the unity of the Spirit, this can be accomplished and God will be well pleased. Embrace them and pray, and the devil's rights will be voided.

You must immediately implement a Bible study program for your children beginning the next day. You must get them to talk and share their feelings in order to gain their trust. This is crucial to turning the tide of the home toward the spiritual realities of God.

I am surprised at the number of Christian parents who allow their children to listen to secular music. There are spiritual repercussions for deliberately allowing demonic spirits to come into your home, but more so, into the spirit of your child. Video games, junk food, and aimless movies all portray one message-REBELLION!

It is the father's responsibility to implement God's order with understanding. Let your children write the words of the lyrics, then go to the word of God and determine the results of such lyrics. Show your daughter how the devil persists at trying to get her pregnant first in the mind through songs and physical rhythms that produce strongholds. Reveal how he wants your sons to produce children without realizing that they are potentially procreating bastards. Help them understand that repercussions will follow them all their life. Show them the benefits of waiting for marriage and building a family that will continue the purposes of God throughout the family's generations to follow.

If you give understanding, your children will understand and accept why you place these decrees before them and live by them without compromise. Most of all, they will notice that *you* have changed in areas of your life. They will observe that you are sensitive about what you put before your eyes and ears and that unhealthy food is not part of your general diet. This is precisely why children act as bastards even though their father is at home. He is there, but the instructions of everyday living unto the Lord are not to be found.

A WORD TO MOTHERS

Your sensitivity toward your children is understood. You carried them inside of your womb for nine months. They fed from your breast for up to three years. There is just something about disciplining your child that might not "feel" right in your heart. Well, this being the case, God has provided a word of insight for you to understand the results of raising your child the way you "feel" instead of the way it is written:

84

Pro 30:11 There is a generation that curseth their father, and doth not bless their mother.

Pro 19:18 Chasten thy son while there is hope, and let not thy soul spare for his crying.

You must stand with your husband as he trains and disciplines his seed and the fruit of your womb. They will indeed run to you to avoid the confrontation of the authority in the home, but you must remember that you are joined together by God as one flesh with your husband, not with your children. Of a truth, your tenderness, affection, and maternal instincts are critical in smoothing out the rough edges during the process of the "fathering process." Be sensitive and discerning as to how and when you allow your role to operate. One key word to bear in mind is "temperance." In doing so, you will be effective as the mother that God made you to be.

5 FATHERS OF OUR CHURCHES

I f people were asked what they expected from their pastors, they would not really say much beyond teaching the Bible, conducting their funeral and simply reassuring them that God understands. Yet more and more laity are showing increasing dissatisfaction with their pastor stating that they are not being taught the Word, or that a clear purpose for the church is lacking in a spiritual sense. When problems arise in the life of a member and there has been no true preparation that goes beyond Sunday, Wednesday and Friday night service, the reality of leadership really comes home.

The concept of father in our churches has become a profession of words and not a position proved by fruit. Most have become a paid piper and not a man separated unto God to declare what the Spirit of God is saying to His people in a relevant way. In essence, our desired leadership reflects the temptations of our hearts. We are tempted to select leaders based on the lust of the flesh and not as one led by the love of God's Spirit. We want to be religious and not spiritual. We want to feel good and not feel right. We want to be tolerated and not agitated. So we choose the Saul's and not the David's.

Today there are "Samuel's" praying and crying to God because they feel rejected by mainstream Christianity. Stop praying! They haven't rejected you. They have rejected God.

> *1 Sam 8:6,7 But the thing displeased Samuel, when they said, Give us a king to judge us. And Samuel prayed unto the LORD. And the LORD said unto Samuel, Hearken unto the voice of the people in all that they say unto thee: for they have not rejected thee, but they have rejected me, that I should not reign over them.*

Church leadership has become a taskmaster over God's heritage by demanding conformity to programs and structures that have little or no relevance for God's agenda. Pastors whose hearts are after the possessions of the people and not after the people, surround themselves with unnecessary props including men who are unlearned in the Scriptures so as not to oppose questionable practices and ulterior motives. Yet, they would not seek out those men who discern by the Spirit of God, and would, in love, confront compromise and self-interest.

> *2 Cor 12:14 Behold, the third time I am ready to come to you; and I will not be burdensome to you: for I seek not yours, but you: for the children ought not to lay up for the parents, but the parents for the children.*

Such men are those who started in the faith but became shipwrecked, as well as those who altogether entered in by some other way.

> *1 Tim 1:19 Holding faith, and a good conscience; which some having put away concerning faith have made shipwreck:*

> *John 10:1 Verily, verily, I say unto you, He that entereth not by the door into the sheepfold, but climbeth up some other way, the same is a thief and a robber.*

The former is worse than the latter because they knew the way of righteousness, but turned their back on such a sacred command (2 Pet. 2:21,22).

Isaiah, Jeremiah, and Ezekiel were all familiar with kings and priests who rejected God's counsel. For some evasive reason, we believe the word they spoke was for their time and day, not ours. Let us be reminded that not only were these things written aforetime for our learning (Rom. 15:4), but that all Scripture is profitable for doctrine, for reproof, for correction, for instruction in righteousness so that the man of God may be perfect (in his ways) and completely furnished (with examples of God), unto all good works (2 Tim. 3:16,17).

Preachers in general, whether they are pastors, prophets, evangelists, apostles, or teachers, have shied away from defending the Gospel against impostors, not New Agers, for they are obvious. They have shied away from those who profess Jesus, yet practice deceit; those who err and are not confronted by men full of the Holy Ghost and boldness.

> *Acts 5:3 But Peter said, Ananias, why hath satan filled thine heart to lie to the Holy Ghost, and to keep back part of the price of the land?*

> *Gal 2:4 And that because of false brethren unawares brought in, who came in privily to spy out our liberty which we have in Christ Jesus, that they might bring us into bondage:*

> *Gal 2:11 But when Peter was come to Antioch, I withstood him to the face, because he was to be blamed.*

We have become respecters of persons and fearful of man whose breath is in his nostrils. We have, through covetousness, desired to keep peace with mere flesh instead of keeping peace with God who is a Consuming Fire.

> *Jer 6:14 They have healed also the hurt of the daughter of my people slightly, saying, Peace, peace; when there is no peace.*

Regardless of how hard men try to organize God out, He is still in! Never mind how well the network is secured and set up, if it is not dependent upon the arm of the Lord, it will falter and fail. This is the very fear of those who refuse to declare the whole counsel of God!

> *Psa 20:6, 7 Now know I that the LORD saveth his anointed; he will hear him from his holy heaven with the saving strength of his right hand. Some trust in chariots, and some in horses: but we will remember the name of the LORD our God.*

Contempt toward God is obvious when men assume to approve one man over the other. It is a witness against those leaders that are unable to discern the man of God by the Spirit of God, and yet they classify themselves as one who walks with God!

We sound like the scribes who questioned Jesus:

> *Mk 11:28 And say unto him, By what authority doest thou these things? and who gave thee this authority to do these things?*

While it is very important that we seek the witness of others in accordance with godly order, may we yet realize that it is God that must yet grant us witness to His will concerning people.

The "system" can never tell what is of God for it is marred with flesh and with the leaven of the scribes and Pharisees. We were cautioned to beware of it yet we go on believing their lies because of the hardness of our hearts. Therefore, we are deceived.

Our pulpits are full of unchastised sons, bastards who refuse the ways and dealings of God in their character. They want to preach the word, but they do not want to be conformed to it. They do not want to be salted with fire and purged and purified that they may be partakers of His holiness.

Am I coming across as disrespectful toward our leadership? Perhaps toward leadership that is appointed by men, but of those that have been appointed by God, no. We must understand that when leadership is leading in the direction of permissive covetousness and that the "vision" originates from their own heart, God will raise up a voice against it! He will herald a voice that cannot be controlled by Jezebel and those that eat at her table, for such are unable to stand for the Lord. They are clouds without rain, full of vanities.

God is using those who have been enabled by His grace to face the religious order of their generation as He used the prophets of old such as:

• Elijah, who confronted Ahab without regard for his position as king.

• Jeremiah, who said, "Thus saith the Lord" even though he had to face 40–50 years of intense suffering at the hands of kings Josiah, Jehoiakim, and Zedekiah.

• Ezekiel, who resounded, "Thus saith Jehovah" repeatedly despite the determination of God's people to continue in their rebellion.

• Isaiah, who tore into the hypocritical system without reservation of men's opinion and objections and sealed his testimony by being sawed in two.

• Our Lord, Jesus Christ, who confronted the powers to be and labeled them serpents and generation of vipers (Matt. 23:33). He went as far as to notify them that their father was the devil himself (John 8:44). For even as lucifer rejected God as his creator, he now tempts men to reject God as their Father.

Time would fail me to bring attention to the fact that it was not Rome who tried to kill Jesus - it was His own people. Poor Pilate tried to set Him free. It was not the Gentiles who beat Paul - it was the Jews that stirred up the people. And today, it is not Hollywood or Congress at the helm. It is the system-the sons of the scribes and Pharisees who fill up the measure of their fathers (Matt. 23:32).

Those who reject the above examples alongside many others, have caused the people of God to yield to secularism. Because of this, they are unable to discern right from wrong, or good from bad. And what is the fruit of it all? To begin with, a powerless word and a faint hearted commitment. Following is the inability to partake of strong meat and repetitiously laying again the foundation of repentance from dead works and of faith toward God and of all the principle doctrines of Christ (Heb. 6:1).

Thus has God's flock been scattered and His people led astray.

Jer 23:2 Therefore thus saith the LORD God of Israel against the pastors that feed my people; Ye have scattered my flock, and driven them away, and have not visited them: behold, I will visit upon you the evil of your doings, saith the LORD.

Jer 50:6 My people hath been lost sheep: their shepherds have caused them to go astray, they have turned them away on the mountains: they have gone from mountain to hill, they have forgotten their resting place.

Isa 56:10, 11 His watchmen are blind: they are all igno-rant, they are all dumb dogs, they cannot bark; sleeping, lying down, loving to slumber. Yea, they are greedy dogs which can never have enough, and they are shepherds that cannot un-derstand: they all look to their own way, every one for his gain, from his quarter.

Nonetheless, in the midst of such conditions, God has a remnant. Praise God! In the midst of compromise, there is yet conviction stirring in the hearts of those in whom there is no guile (John 1:47). As well, there is yet hope for the prodigal and the rebellious who have pierced themselves through with many sorrows, if only they would repent and return to God's standard.

I am speaking a word that Paul, Peter, John and others have tire-lessly spoken to the Church. That word is, "Take heed! Beware! I warn you! Repent! Return! From such, turn away."

Acts 20:26–31 Wherefore I take you to record this day, that I am pure from the blood of all men. For I have not shunned to declare unto you all the counsel of God. Take heed therefore unto yourselves, and to all the flock, over the which the Holy Ghost hath made you overseers, to feed the church of God, which he hath purchased with his own blood. For I know this, that after my departing shall grievous wolves enter in among you, not sparing the flock. Also of your own selves shall men arise, speaking perverse things, to draw away disciples after them. Therefore watch, and remember, that by the space of three years I ceased not to warn every one night and day with tears.

1 John 4:1 Beloved, believe not every spirit, but try the spirits whether they are of God: because many false prophets are gone out into the world.

I could refer you to Scripture references from Genesis to Revela-tion regarding the truth of our plight in Christianity and its leaders,

93

but the point is that God will no longer wink at the rebellion of the Gentiles. Even as He cut off the Jews, and that for a season until the fullness of the Gentiles comes in (Rom. 11:25), do understand that He is about to cut off those Gentiles who have defiled His vineyard and are doing despite to the blood of His covenant with us through Christ.

> *Rom. 11:21–23 For if God spared not natural branches, take heed lest he also spare not thee. Behold therefore the goodness and severity of God: on them which fell, severity; but toward thee, goodness, if thou continue in his goodness: otherwise thou also shalt be cut off. And they also, if they abide not still in unbelief, shall be grafted in: for God is able to graft them in again.*

Venomous doctrines abound that attempt to remove and totally eliminate godly soberness and a readiness of mind from God's flock. The purpose of soberness is that one may be ready to turn away from all disobedience that is a weight and a hindrance to your spirit (Heb 13:1). The shunning of disobedience can only occur when your obedience is fulfilled. How shall this occur if, regardless of how you live, God does not retain the right or power to discipline? The nation of Israel refused their Father's chastening to the extent of being cut off in order that we might be grafted in. If God has dealt with the natural branch in such a way, let us, being a wild one, take heed and fear. In essence, one is implying that God can be mocked although Scripture clearly states that He cannot-and will not!

> *2 Cor 10:6 And having in a readiness to revenge all disobedience, when your obedience is fulfilled.*

> *2 Pet 2:20 For if after they have escaped the pollutions of the world through the knowledge of the Lord and Saviour*

Jesus Christ, they are again entangled therein, and overcome, the latter end is worse with them than the beginning.

Gal 6:7 Be not deceived; God is not mocked: for whatsoever a man soweth, that shall he also reap.

Furthermore, it is not the hearers of the law that are justified, but the doers (Rom. 2:13), for how would God judge the world if my unrighteousness commended the righteousness of God (Rom. 3:5-7)? How would He separate the wheat from the chaff if the wheat brought forth chaff?

Are not the Scriptures emphatically clear? And yet those whose hearts have not submitted to His Lordship cannot see nor hear, lest their sins be forgiven them. Only God can open your eyes to understand the truth of the holy Scriptures.

Mark 4:11, 12 And he said unto them, Unto you it is given to know the mystery of the kingdom of God: but unto them that are without, all these things are done in parables: That seeing they may see, and not perceive; and hearing they may hear, and not understand; lest at any time they should be converted, and their sins should be forgiven them.

Fellow brother or sister in the faith, Christianity has been ravaged by impostors and our pulpits are not safe anymore. Even though Christianity has always had its share of deceivers, it is reaching last day proportions as prophesied by Our Lord.

Mark 13:5, 6 And Jesus answering them began to say, Take heed lest any man deceive you: For many shall come in my name, saying, I am Christ; and shall deceive many.

The fathers of our churches must be seen even as we are: flesh. We have exalted men out of measure and as a result, there exists two classes of people in the church - clergy and laity. Naturally, we are to esteem our leaders and respect them as unto the Lord, however, when the appearance of godliness is used to cloak our desire to be seen of men, then we have abused our position in the church. This is because our hearts have "persons in admiration." As Paul stated, we desire to glory in the flesh of others.

> *Gal 6:13 For neither they themselves who are circumcised keep the law; but desire to have you circumcised, that they may glory in your flesh.*

> *Jude16 These are murmurers, complainers, walking after their own lusts; and their mouth speaketh great swelling words, having men's persons in admiration because of advantage.*

Heaven will not be the result of a person who followed a man. It will be the result of those who followed after the Christ in men.

The New Testament is almost always exalted for the grace that it reveals. However, there is a lack of warnings and teachings against falsehood and of those who would make merchandise of God's people. It is written:

> *2 Pet 2:3 And through covetousness shall they with feigned words make merchandise of you: whose judgment now of a long time lingereth not, and their damnation slumbereth not.*

In many ways, we have omitted Scriptures that bring conviction and godly fear. Compassion and unmerited grace is the highlight of most preaching and it has remained the focus of many preachers' sermons. There is always a call for the unsaved and those ignorant of God's love toward them. However, we have humanized the Gospel into a social philosophy by having an "appearance" of wisdom, yet lacking the power necessary to transform character and convict those who know the truth but do it not. This is the result when we fail to preach the woes and judgment of God, having more respect toward grace and love, which, in essence, is not the grace and love of the Scriptures, but that which is of the flesh when presented unqualified.

> *Col 2:18–23 Let no man beguile you of your reward in a voluntary humility and worshipping of angels, intruding into those things which he hath not seen, vainly puffed up by his fleshly mind, And not holding the Head, from which all the body by joints and bands having nourishment ministered, and knit together, increaseth with the increase of God. Wherefore if ye be dead with Christ from the rudiments of the world, why, as though living in the world, are ye subject to ordinances, (Touch not; taste not; handle not; Which all are to perish with the using;) after the commandments and doctrines of men? Which things have indeed a shew of wisdom in will worship, and humility, and neglecting of the body; not in any honour to the satisfying of the flesh.*

Many ministries thrive off messages of peace, love, joy, (of course, faith), social justice, self–acceptance, and forms of humanism when a word of repentance and holiness is called for. Materialism and sex have clothed themselves in the religious garb of prosperity and self esteem to entangle the simple minded into many hurtful lusts and ineffective service for God's kingdom. We are entertaining motivational as well as social celebrities whose god is not the Lord. Such unholy alliances shall fall and those who have yielded to such relationships after the flesh and the honor of men will be evident by the piercing through of their soul with many sorrows that is upon them.

> *1 Tim 6:9, 10 But they that will be rich fall into temptation and a snare, and into many foolish and hurtful lusts, which drown men in destruction and perdition. For the love*

of money is the root of all evil: which while some coveted after, they have erred from the faith, and pierced themselves through with many sorrows.

Such spirits of control and fertility have pressed themselves upon the will of man and have replaced the desire for God's Spirit in our lives. The urge for growth and expansion has bred a competitive spirit that will be confronted by God in a most profound way. Today's ministers must have an invested interest if they are going to support your work financially. Without directly saying, (then again some do), "What's in it for me?" The spirit of control and power strategies exist to ensure that they get their "blessing."

When we look closely into this, we begin to realize that it is the same desire that had its conception in the Garden of Eden. The desire was for more than what God had given.

This mentality has given birth to financial institutions that lend billions to Christian organizations who are looking for money in an attempt to buy the glory. We have ignored God's protocol for financing His work. The tithe that is so aggressively preached is collected and given to those institutions that church leadership has become servant to. While borrowing money to expand the work of God is not necessarily wrong in and of itself, it must be pursued with soberness and caution. It should be the will of God as much as anything else. A person's motive can certainly make it an idol. Crunching numbers and running corporate estimations for elaborate buildings will not usher the glory of God any closer to you. Your body is the temple of the Holy Ghost, not your building. Many times, these are attempts to replace an absentee personal relationship with the Lord.

98

1 Cor 6:20 For ye are bought with a price: therefore glorify God in your body, and in your spirit, which are God's.

Paul clearly states that there would not be many fathers who would genuinely care for us, but there would be ten thousand teachers who would desire to instruct us.

> *1 Cor 4:15 For though ye have ten thousand instructors in Christ, yet have ye not many fathers: for in Christ Jesus I have begotten you through the gospel.*

Despite all the disarray and systems that have perpetrated the lives of our leadership, there are yet sincere and God fearing men who are standing their ground. God has called them forth, and they are determined to remain true to His call and His standard of righteousness and holiness.

God has a remnant within this system who are praying for His wind to blow and bring restoration of relationship with Him. Anyone who understands restoration will tell you that before it comes, judgment comes. If it did not, people would be judged without having had an opportunity to judge themselves. Though we rebel, God always sends a warning to His people to get their house in order.

This remnant of saints, unknown to man but known by God, are preparing while abiding in "caves." They are praying and fasting for God to arise and work. They have sacrificed jobs of security and positions of popularity to truly know what the Spirit of the Lord is saying. They are not satisfied with normality and the mixture of the leaven in the things of God. They want the fullness of God in them for their own salvation, rather than for His people. This causes them to walk soberly and without respect of persons. Many, likewise, will one day leave the very churches that they have been members at for years. When God speaks, they are going to be released to move where God is calling them.

I believe the fathers of our churches are waking up to the realization that change is needed within the heart for this is God's protocol. Despite all the notions of ministry, of which many have been caught up in, they are yet lonely for the communion of God's Spirit within and upon them. Even those who know the depth of their wrong desire to return to the sincerity of yesterday when they simply desired God.

There remains hope for the one who has cast off the reigns of a loving God. If you feel the pangs of shame and a wave of conviction, God is beckoning you to return home. Though you have the appearance of a successful ministry, are in great demand and can preach a preacher's sermon, it will not replace the sincere heart and truth in the inward parts that God desires and demands.

> *Josh 24:14 Now therefore fear the LORD, and serve him in sincerity and in truth: and put away the gods which your fathers served on the other side of the flood, and in Egypt; and serve ye the LORD.*

Both laity and clergy within the Body of Christ must understand that if God can use a donkey, then He certainly can accomplish His will without us. Though He can, He doesn't. He has made man a copartner to herald the message of salvation. A realization must occur to leadership that God is going to get His way by decreeing a new move of His Spirit upon leadership that has not and will not bow their knee to the baals of our generation. The end justifying the means is an excuse that will not be tolerated by the Joshua generation who is awakening to a militant battle in the spiritual realm.

100

With all boldness, I warn and encourage all those in leadership positions to search themselves! Oh, the dealings of God upon those who have done despite to His people bears an eternal weight that one will not want to experience. This is why the force of this book is heavy and plain of speech without respect of persons. God does not wish for any man to be lost under such a state.

>*Eze 3:17, 18,20,21 Son of man, I have made thee a watchman unto the house of Israel: therefore hear the word at my mouth, and give them warning from me. When I say unto the wicked, Thou shalt surely die; and thou givest him not warning, nor speakest to warn the wicked from his wicked way, to save his life; the same wicked man shall die in his iniquity; but his blood will I require at thine hand. Again, When a righteous man doth turn from his righteousness, and commit iniquity, and I lay a stumblingblock before him, he shall die: because thou hast not given him warning, he shall die in his sin, and his righteousness which he hath done shall not be remembered; but his blood will I require at thine hand. Nevertheless, if thou warn the righteous man, that the righteous sin not, and he doth not sin, he shall surely live, because he is warned; also thou hast delivered thy soul.*

With sober minds, let us grasp the spiritual weight of this truth; man's majority counts for nothing before God.

We, as men, have tripped over each other at one time or another by walking more so with flesh than with God. It is through such insecurities that we have yielded to the flattery of self–ambition and have compromised at declaring all of God's counsel. We have hearkened more to the concern of people's emotions than God's demands. Therefore, we are snared by persuasion that does not come from above.

>*Gal 5:7–9 Ye did run well; who did hinder you that ye should not obey the truth? This persuasion cometh not of him that calleth you. A little leaven leaveneth the whole lump.*

As men, we desire and seek the approval of men. This is every bit natural. However, it is when we seek the approval of men that we discover problems. It is God's responsibility to approve His word through the men He chooses. We are not to go searching for it. If, through patience, we wait for God, confirmation will come. But if, through our own internal insecurities, we beseech the comfort of others, we will always be unclear and uncertain about His will. It is through such thinking that we dangerously open ourselves to knowing men after the flesh and, in doing so, expose ourselves to the weakness of others. If not wise, we can be overtaken in their fault (Gal. 6:1).

Many of our fathers or those in leadership positions have coined a phrase that sounds good but is unfounded in the Scriptures: "I haven't sat under your ministry."

Now, there is nothing wrong with needing to qualify the authenticity of ones ministry, but let us not get religious. Who has the time to sit under everyone's ministry? This is not God's protocol in knowing if one is of God or of themselves.

1 John 4:1 Beloved, believe not every spirit, but try the spirits whether they are of God: because many false prophets are gone out into the world.

Eph 5:10 Proving what is acceptable unto the Lord.

God has given us clear and concise measures to know those that are of Him and those that are of themselves, yet when time is not spent before God and His word, the proving of things and people by the Spirit is not as clear as we would want it to be. When we pursue knowledge through courses and classes without our motives and desires being purified, we are yet found without a quickening of His Spirit to know His perfect will.

102

Heb 8:11 And they shall not teach every man his neighbour, and every man his brother, saying, Know the Lord: for all shall know me, from the least to the greatest.

1 John 2:27 But the anointing which ye have received of him abideth in you, and ye need not that any man teach you: but as the same anointing teacheth you of all things, and is truth, and is no lie, and even as it hath taught you, ye shall abide in him.

1 Cor 2:10 But God hath revealed them unto us by his Spirit: for the Spirit searcheth all things, yea, the deep things of God.

There is a reason for the condition of every relationship. We can tell when our cars need repairs. We can perceive when our hot water tank is no longer producing hot water. Even so, God has also allowed us to discern when our relationships are breaking down as men, as women, as families, and with those in the ministry. Inevitably, we must seek to rebuild broken relationships in order for us to maintain a clear and concise view of God and His Kingdom. To ignore them is to forfeit an opportunity to experience the excellency of God's ways while knowing the fruitful relationships amongst others that can only be experienced through returning to our first love. It simply is a healthy part of spiritual life that must unfold.

There are reasons for any breakdown and we must realize that in our generation of ministers, it is far too common, nor is it the will and way of God. Let us simply repair and restore these vital relationships that prove us to be sons and not bastards.

6 BREAKDOWN OF RELATIONSHIPS

The whole breakdown of church leadership, whether great or small, is found within the breakdown of relationship. While being careful not to throw the baby out with the bath water or to judge in a spirit of condemnation, we must yet judge the fruit of our doings and provide an honest assessment of our condition.

Our relationship with God means that we are to become established as confirmed in Scripture by the examples of our High Priest, Jesus Christ. Any other means will not accomplish His purpose in us as effective vessels. We have adopted the way of knowledge to replace the way of the cross and the way of seminary to replace the way of our cemetery. In essence, we have rejected the way of self–abasement that is necessary to know God. We have believed that we can follow Christ without a cross. We attempt to replace His order with a degree or a ministry that we inherit from a parent or denomination. We have greatly erred.

Men who have not been chastised or purged are finding their way into the pulpits of our churches. No longer is the life of Christ the standard by which we judge ourselves as leaders. Rather, we cleave to the standard of traditions and ordinances that indeed possess Scripture yet have little or no spiritual aptitude. Such ideologies indeed appear to be wise yet they are void of power and conviction because they are void of God's presence and approval.

> *Col 2:8 Beware lest any man spoil you through philosophy and vain deceit, after the tradition of men, after the rudiments of the world, and not after Christ.*

The exposure of church leadership is not over. Those few that have been exposed on a national level cannot be compared to those who are yet showing contempt toward the Lord. We are taken aback when we hear of child molesters operating our day care centers, fornicators posing as youth pastors, and womanizers and adulterers leading as pastors. The spirit of homosexuality is accepted at large in most denominations, and lesbianism is more prevalent than we would care to admit.

We have replaced the leading of God's Spirit with letters of approval or works, which cannot replace fruit. Anyone can build a ministry with money, but only God can build one by His Spirit. Such a person thinks they can purchase the things of God even as Simon.

> *Acts 8:20,21 But Peter said unto him, Thy money perish with thee, because thou hast thought that the gift of God may be purchased with money. Thou hast neither part nor lot in this matter: for thy heart is not right in the sight of God.*

106 CHRIST—OUR STANDARD

> *Phil 2:5–7 Let this mind be in you, which was also in Christ Jesus: Who, being in the form of God, thought it not*

robbery to be equal with God: But made himself of no reputa-
tion, and took upon him the form of a servant, and was made
in the likeness of men:

When we behold the person of Jesus, many of us fail to see what He endured in order to become who He is. He did not just appear on the scene speaking eloquently while angels manicured His nails. He did not float through Jerusalem and say, "I am the Son of God." The first thing He did was make Himself of no reputation by removing His garment of glory, and embracing the attire of a servant. He was found in fashion of a man although He is completely God. Even in this, He did not appear as man on the earth instantaneously. He was born naturally (however, born of a virgin), and in doing so, fulfilled all righteousness in relationship with man.

If He had denied becoming a man from the womb and living everyday life as a man, He would not be found qualified to die for mankind or even intercede on our behalf. Though this seems contrary to our thoughts about God, it is not. The one thing God did not know was what it was like to be a man faced with temptation. Not until He became flesh and encountered man's frailties could He be qualified to truly taste death for every man. To make the Captain of our soul perfect, this had to be accomplished through the sufferings of Jesus that He may be touched by the feelings of our infirmities.

> *Heb 2:9,10 But we see Jesus, who was made a little lower*
> *than the angels for the suffering of death, crowned with glory*
> *and honour; that he by the grace of God should taste death for*
> *every man. For it became him, for whom are all things, and*
> *by whom are all things, in bringing many sons unto glory, to*
> *make the captain of their salvation perfect through sufferings.*

As human beings, we would not experience what we experience as Christians if Christ had not conformed to our nature as human beings. If He had purposed to save the angels who had lost their first estate, He would have had to become an angel (Heb. 2:16). Instead, He chose to redeem man who was made a little lower than the angels (Heb. 2:7). He was fashioned as unto us (Heb. 2:14) yet without sin, that He might reconcile us to relationship unto Himself through the cross of His death of which we all must partake. This is why He is not ashamed to call us brethren.

> *Heb 2:11 For both he that sanctifieth and they who are sanctified are all of one: for which cause he is not ashamed to call them brethren,*

The reality of His being made like unto His brethren also contains within it the power of His effective ministry of High Priest. In essence, had Jesus the man *not* endured chastening but instead, refused to submit to His Father's will, He would be found to be an illegitimate Son - yes, a bastard. But thank God He is not, "for in all things it behooved Him to be made like unto His brethren, that He might be a merciful and faithful High Priest in things pertaining to God, to make reconciliation for the sins of the people" (Heb. 2:17).

Throughout His entire ministry, His effectiveness over satan and within men was always associated with pleasing His Father rather than Himself or His bride.

> *Matt 3:17 And lo a voice from heaven, saying, This is my beloved Son, in whom I am well pleased.*

> *Luke 2:49 And he said unto them, How is it that ye sought me? wist ye not that I must be about my Father's business?*

John 5:17 But Jesus answered them, My Father worketh hitherto, and I work.

John 8:29 And he that sent me is with me: the Father hath not left me alone; for I do always those things that please him.

Relationship with His Father made His life effective and equipped Him to minister to mankind. His relationship bore fruit, not His knowledge or power. Knowledge and power followed after because it flowed as a result of a solid relationship built on obedience and conformity to the character of His Father.

Jesus had to learn obedience as a man through what He suffered! He already knew how to be God.

Heb 5:7, 8 Who in the days of his flesh, when he had offered up prayers and supplications with strong crying and tears unto him that was able to save him from death, and was heard in that he feared, Though he were a Son, yet learned he obedience by the things which he suffered;

The role of High Priest was not just handed to Jesus. He earned it not just with His death, but also with His life. In fact, His death was acceptable because His life was. If His life had been a demonstration of fulfilling God's purpose for our salvation in His own way, then our salvation would be built on rebellion. Thus, we would have an excuse to dwell in sin, for Christ Himself would have sinned (of which it was impossible, for He had no sin in Him).

109

SATAN'S MISSION: PRODUCE BASTARDS

After one makes a reasonable assessment of satan and his kingdom agenda, a vivid view of his purpose should become obvious, or as we understand it today, his mission statement will become clear. We must not complicate who satan is and what he is after. He is a deceiver, a liar and an impostor. He is after the sons of God. He is after that which he does not have. He likewise recognizes that his success is not determined by his power to overthrow us through some manifested show of power.

His success is secured by default of our own decision to forfeit the requirements of God. This is why though the seeds were sown on four types of soil, only one type produced fruit; that which is good soil. Only one was true. Only one was legitimate. The other forms of soil proved to be bastards because they refused to be conformed, to continue, to endure or to deny themselves until they be made fit for the Master's use. No matter the reason, they did not overcome. The reasons were not found in the seed that was sown. Rather, it was found in the condition of the heart.

Satan's objective is to make men to bear illegitimate fruit while allowing them to maintain an idea of acceptance by mere confession.

We see this revealed in this disclosure when the tempter came to our Lord. He came with doubt and question by stating "if" thou be the Son of God. The whole thrust of his approach was to separate Jesus from His Father. He was willing to give up the world in order to simply get to the Son. Even today, satan will give you fame, ministries, money, and pleasures in abundance to keep you from truly being and continually becoming a son of God, conformed to the image of His dear Son, Jesus.

110

> *Matt 4:3–11 And when the tempter came to him, he said, If thou be the Son of God, command that these stones be made bread. But he answered and said, It is written, Man shall not live by bread alone, but by every word that proceedeth*

out of the mouth of God. Then the devil taketh him up into the holy city, and setteth him on a pinnacle of the temple, And saith unto him, If thou be the Son of God, cast thyself down: for it is written, He shall give his angels charge concerning thee: and in their hands they shall bear thee up, lest at any time thou dash thy foot against a stone. Jesus said unto him, It is written again, Thou shalt not tempt the Lord thy God. Again, the devil taketh him up into an exceeding high mountain, and sheweth him all the kingdoms of the world, and the glory of them; And saith unto him, All these things will I give thee, if thou wilt fall down and worship me. Then saith Jesus unto him, Get thee hence, Satan: for it is written, Thou shalt worship the Lord thy God, and him only shalt thou serve. Then the devil leaveth him, and, behold, angels came and ministered unto him.

Gen 3:4–6 And the serpent said unto the woman, Ye shall not surely die: For God doth know that in the day ye eat thereof, then your eyes shall be opened, and ye shall be as gods, knowing good and evil. And when the woman saw that the tree was good for food, and that it was pleasant to the eyes, and a tree to be desired to make one wise, she took of the fruit thereof, and did eat, and gave also unto her husband with her; and he did eat.

From the first time that Jesus entered into satan's realm, satan attempted to kill Him physically. When he realized that he could not accomplish this, his second attempt was to break His relationship with God. This was the same temptation that Adam yielded to and blamed his wife for, though indirectly, Adam was totally blaming God.

Gen 3:12 And the man said, The woman whom thou gavest to be with me, she gave me of the tree, and I did eat.

Adam's words may have been, "If You, God, did not give me this woman, I would have never done this." It is the nature of man to blame God indirectly from his mouth, while in his heart, he is directly blaming God.

To completely understand the totality of Jesus' ministry over satan, we must comprehend by the Spirit exactly what Jesus endured just prior to His temptation.

If we recall the Scripture correctly, He had just completed a 40 day and night fast and He was hungry (Matt. 4:2). He totally emptied Himself of physical strength, and it was during the lowest point of weakness that He showed the highest form of obedience. We fail to realize that Jesus as God never knew what it was like to feel hungry until He was driven into the wilderness to be tempted of the devil as a man.

When Jesus, as a complete man, demonstrated complete obedience under circumstances that no other man will ever know, He was making a declaration to all who would accept Him as Lord and Savior. He was declaring that you cannot obey God until you totally choose to bring the depth of your being under His rule. This only happens when we are broken through trials, suffering and persecution.

Heb 12:3, 4 For consider him that endured such contradiction of sinners against himself, lest ye be wearied and faint in your minds. Ye have not yet resisted unto blood, striving against sin.

The problem that men of God are facing today is that we are not looking unto Jesus when the tempter comes to make us bastards. The devil does not care about how much faith you have, how much power you have, or even how much money you have. His biggest threat is how obedient you are to your Father in heaven!

It was not the attributes of Jesus that pleased God. It was His obedience to God had taught Him to do and speak.

> *John 8:28, 29 Then said Jesus unto them, When ye have lifted up the Son of man, then shall ye know that I am he, and that I do nothing of myself; but as my Father hath taught me, I speak these things. And he that sent me is with me: the Father hath not left me alone; for I do always those things that please him.*

The very act of obedience was the single most vital accomplishment that Jesus achieved. Even when God had forsaken Him, Jesus yet remained obedient unto the death of the cross.

> *Phil 2:8 And being found in fashion as a man, he humbled himself, and became obedient unto death, even the death of the cross.*

Throughout all of the Old Testament, the one thing that God was bringing to an end was disobedience. His most passionate heartbeat then and even now was to have a people that would obey His voice during the wilderness times of their lives as well as the peaks. Time after time, He spoke through His prophets of old when the day would come that He would give us a heart of flesh, and write His commandments upon them that we would simply obey His voice.

> *Exo 19:5 Now therefore, if ye will obey my voice indeed, and keep my covenant, then ye shall be a peculiar treasure unto me above all people: for all the earth is mine:*

> *Isa 59:21 As for me, this is my covenant with them, saith the LORD; My spirit that is upon thee, and my words which I have put in thy mouth, shall not depart out of thy mouth, nor out of the mouth of thy seed, nor out of the mouth of thy seed's seed, saith the LORD, from henceforth and for ever.*

Isa 61:8, 9 For I the LORD love judgment, I hate rob-bery for burnt offering; and I will direct their work in truth, and I will make an everlasting covenant with them. And their seed shall be known among the Gentiles, and their offspring among the people: all that see them shall acknowledge them, that they are the seed which the LORD hath blessed.

Ezek 11:19 And I will give them one heart, and I will put a new spirit within you; and I will take the stony heart out of their flesh, and will give them an heart of flesh:

Allow me to reiterate that Jesus did not know obedience as a man until He descended on earth through the Virgin Mary. For the next thirty–three years, He learned obedience in order to be qualified as an obedient sacrifice, not one that contained blemishes of rebellion. I will go as far as to say that had Christ not lived an obedient life, His blood would not have been perfect as an atonement for our sins. It was not just the blood of God that made the cross effective; it was the obedient man that allowed His pre-qualified blood to fulfill its mission; wash away our sins.

Hence, we see within the life of Christ that satan's ultimate objective was to wedge disobedience between man and God. You ask, "Disobedience to what?" To which I answer, "To conforming to the likeness of His Son."

Rom 8:29 For whom he did foreknow, he also did predes-tinate to be conformed to the image of his Son, that he might be the firstborn among many brethren.

2 Pet 1:4 Whereby are given unto us exceeding great and precious promises: that by these ye might be partakers of the divine nature, having escaped the corruption that is in the world through lust.

Eph 4:24 And that ye put on the new man, which after God is created in righteousness and true holiness.

Today's microwave religion and mega marketing efforts are losing sight of what really matters. God's glory will not draw near to illegitimate sons, no matter how large the crowds. We can go through all the rituals, give our sacrifices and double tithes as well as visit every conference around the globe. It is not until we stand before God Almighty and release totally ourselves to His refining fire, that we will be fit to bring forth the peaceable fruit of righteousness.

A bastard is produced when a son will not hearken to the correction of his heavenly Father. A heathen cannot be a bastard because he is not a son of God. A bastard occurs when God's chastisement and rebuking is being rejected by His own, and the choice to hold onto the idols in our life prevail, that we label ourselves, "illegitimate children." This very issue causes many Christians to remain children in the faith, rather than pressing toward becoming young men and women of the faith, and ultimately, faithful fathers and mothers.

This process from son to bastard cannot be isolated to a specific timetable. God alone is Father and He alone knows the true condition of His son's heart. However, once a son is no longer bearing fruit of the Spirit and possessing a spirit of reverence toward God and man, he is confirming his own state of being.

2 Pet 2:10 But chiefly them that walk after the flesh in the lust of uncleanness, and despise government. Presumptuous are they, selfwilled, they are not afraid to speak evil of dignities.

> *2 Pet 2:14,15 Having eyes full of adultery, and that cannot cease from sin; beguiling unstable souls: an heart they have exercised with covetous practices; cursed children: Which have forsaken the right way, and are gone astray, following the way of Balaam the son of Bosor, who loved the wages of unrighteousness;*

> *2 Pet 2:19 While they promise them liberty, they themselves are the servants of corruption: for of whom a man is overcome, of the same is he brought in bondage.*

BEING CONFORMED

> *Phil 3:7–9 But what things were gain to me, those I counted loss for Christ. Yea doubtless, and I count all things but loss for the excellency of the knowledge of Christ Jesus my Lord: for whom I have suffered the loss of all things, and do count them but dung, that I may win Christ, And be found in him, not having mine own righteousness, which is of the law, but that which is through the faith of Christ, the righteousness which is of God by faith: That I may know him, and the power of his resurrection, and the fellowship of his sufferings, being made conformable unto his death; If by any means I might attain unto the resurrection of the dead.*

Do not ignore the above Scripture for it is the crux of relationship with God.

What inhibits us from perpetually knowing Christ is that we fail to count our righteousness, talents, gifts, ministries and all our positions that are gain to us, as a loss for Christ (v.7). We come to know Him at a certain level, become comfortable and then begin to set up idols. Those idols are the very talents, ministries and the like that He has given us. As a result, we fall short of the excellency of the knowledge of our Lord (v.8).

We wonder why many Christians can never come to maturity and are always in need of crisis counseling. They very seldom can stand when faced with spiritual warfare that comes because of the word's sake. Many other pitfalls are holding God's people back from fighting a good fight of faith. They have yet to count their attributes or relationships that are after the flesh as dung that they may win Christ. He will not share the excellency of His knowledge with one who has not suffered the loss of all things and considers them worthless. Unless we keep this truth ever before us, we will forget and yield to the philosophies of men.

Until we come to the end of ourselves, we, by the same measure, cannot draw near to the beginnings in Christ. This is the painful process of being made conformable to His death (v.10). This is the process of chastisement, correction, discipline, rebuke and the unpopular message of purging with His fire that we may bring forth more fruit.

> *John 15:2 Every branch in me that beareth not fruit he taketh away: and every branch that beareth fruit, he purgeth it, that it may bring forth more fruit.*

Until we have conformed unto His death by our death, we will fail to conform to His life in and through our life. We must not escape through declaring, "It is by faith, brother, that I am conformed to His death, not by works." Well, that is partial truth and here is the rest of the story.

> *Jas 2:18–20,24 Yea, a man may say, Thou hast faith, and I have works: shew me thy faith without thy works, and I will shew thee my faith by my works. Thou believest that there is one God; thou doest well: the devils also believe, and tremble.*

But wilt thou know, O vain man, that faith without works is dead? Ye see then how that by works a man is justified, and not by faith only.

Anytime we interpret the Scriptures to avoid the cross, sufferings, trials and God's chastisement, we are yielding to the flattery of men and the doctrines of devils (1 Tim. 4:1; Col. 2:8). Let us judge after the Spirit and not after the flesh. Whenever a doctrine makes provision for the flesh, that doctrine is not of God.

Ro 8:5 For they that are after the flesh do mind the things of the flesh; but they that are after the Spirit the things of the Spirit.

SOUL PAIN

I understand what it means to experience the pain of the soul. You cannot put your finger on where it hurts. It is a depth of pain that your being undergoes through a massive burning by the Spirit of God as He cleanses, purifies and refines your heart, spirit and understanding.

Until we know the pain of the soul, we cannot speak from the depths of it. This is why the depth of the anointing is synonymous with the depth that God has been allowed to work in our souls.

The pain, fear and anxieties that we feel in our soul are evidence that we yet need the workings of God to conform us to His Son for our spiritual profit.

Heb 12:5–11 And ye have forgotten the exhortation which speaketh unto you as unto children, My son, despise not thou the chastening of the Lord, nor faint when thou art rebuked of him: For whom the Lord loveth he chasteneth, and scourgeth every son whom he receiveth.

If ye endure chastening, God dealeth with you as with sons; for what son is he whom the father chasteneth not? But if ye be without chastisement, whereof all are partakers, then are ye bastards, and not sons. Furthermore we have had fathers of our flesh which corrected us, and we gave them reverence: shall we not much rather be in subjection unto the Father of spirits, and live? For they verily for a few days chastened us after their own pleasure; but he for our profit, that we might be partakers of his holiness. Now no chastening for the present seemeth to be joyous, but grievous: nevertheless afterward it yieldeth the peaceable fruit of righteousness unto them which are exercised thereby.

Please read these verses with a deliberate attention to the whole context of this chapter. Verse one of chapter twelve is dealing with laying aside the sins and weights. Verse two is looking unto Jesus who endured His cross. Verse three restates that we should consider Jesus in order that we do not faint because if He endured His cross, we can endure ours. Verse four tells us that we have not had to wrestle to that of blood, striving against sin. Finally, we come to understand the whole thrust of Hebrews chapter twelve; God is bringing us to a position of character that we might run this race!

Jesus was brought to a position of character as High Priest before He was exalted to the right hand of God as High Priest!

This verse summarizes the pain of our soul, and explains why we are encouraged not to faint when we are rebuked of Him. He whom He loves He chasteneth. Chasten, in the Greek, is "puideu." It means to train, discipline, instruct, or teach. This is what it means to be disciplined. God also "scourgeth every son whom he receiveth." Scourgeth is "mastigoo." It means to flog or to beat. Did not our Lord endure His flogging for our healing? Yes, He did.

Chastening and scourging are not designed to last forever. It lasts for a season and afterwards, yields the peaceable fruit of righteousness! This time of experiencing our soul pain does not feel good but grievous. We must choose to endure by being in subjection unto the Father of our spirits that we will live (v 9) and become holy vessels fit for the Master's use, or we will reject His chastening and be found wanting.

> *2 Tim 2:21 If a man therefore purge himself from these, he shall be a vessel unto honour, sanctified, and meet for the master's use, and prepared unto every good work.*

This is exactly where church leadership is lacking. We receive our call, obtain our ordination from man, receive insights from God and assume we have attained full rights to declare things we have not yet been made perfect in.

Many people have falsely assumed that just because they have been granted a leadership position in their church that they are a leader. The characteristic of their true person is revealed when they are not preaching or operating under the anointing. The fruit of sons who have not been made perfect is evident. The anointing will come due to the sovereignty of God regardless of the vessel, be it donkey, rooster or prophet.

Those who have persisted on journeying down this road to spiritual decay begin to lose God's approval. They become visionaries of religious works and forfeit the vision of God, which is borne out of RELATIONSHIP with Him. Religious works was satan's greatest invention to replace the protocol of relationship with God that is based on transformation of nature; the fallen to the divine. This is why although they had done many wonderful works, Jesus still never knew them (Matt. 7:23).

To the unchastised and immature Christian, it does not appear that way. Everything appears well pleasing to God. But to those who have suffered in the soul, their eyes are opened to the shallowness and feigned motives of all who have not laid down their life to be conformed to the image of Christ on a continual basis.

As people, we are so deceived by our hearts. We fail to remember that many of those who have preached to others will end up as a castaway (1 Cor. 9:27). It would have been better for them not to have known the way of righteousness (2 Pet. 2:20). God will never allow the call of preaching His Gospel to replace His call for sonship by and through chastisement.

1Cor 9:27 But I keep under my body, and bring it into subjection: lest that by any means, when I have preached to others, I myself should be a castaway.

2 Pet 2:20 For if after they have escaped the pollutions of the world through the knowledge of the Lord and Saviour Jesus Christ, they are again entangled therein, and overcome, the latter end is worse with them than the beginning.

Heb 6:4–6 For it is impossible for those who were once enlightened, and have tasted of the heavenly gift, and were made partakers of the Holy Ghost, And have tasted the good word of God, and the powers of the world to come, If they shall fall away, to renew them again unto repentance; seeing they crucify to themselves the Son of God afresh, and put him to an open shame.

On the same token, He will yet allow one who has broken relationship with Him to continue to preach the Gospel although they never knew Him.

7 CONFRONTATION OF RELATIONSHIPS

Matt 7:23 And then will I profess unto them, I never knew you: depart from me, ye that work iniquity.

Eze 3:20 Again, When a righteous man doth turn from his righteousness, and commit iniquity, and I lay a stumblingblock before him, he shall die: because thou hast not given him warning, he shall die in his sin, and his righteousness which he hath done shall not be remembered; but his blood will I require at thine hand.

Do you notice here that the only reason why they felt they should enter into heaven was because of what they did? The issue of ever knowing Christ personally and intimately is totally ignored.

I believe, by the moving of God's Spirit in these last days, that God is going to cause leadership to confront leadership. This issue is heavily ignored. When men whom God has purged begin to cause other men to face the reality of their hearts, God will honor this by providing mercy, causing hearts to turn and repent.

As I finalize this chapter, I do so with a realization that I have not scratched the surface regarding the issue of relationships. Placing it all in perspective is no easy task in practice. It can only come about by:

- Having Christ as our standard.

- Not allowing satan to produce a bastard out of us.

- Understanding the pain of our soul.

- Being vessels for His use.

- Not deceiving ourselves because we are in the pulpit yet not in Him. All such philosophies are based on self righteousness and fall short of producing sons of God.

If you have refused His correction, His teaching and even His flogging to the state of obvious rebellion, your fruit in relationship will certainly reveal your place in name; son or bastard. Which are you?

This brings us to a most crucial and sensitive area of life in ministry with our peers. Peers in ministry are vital. They bring with them a value that we all treasure as well as provide us a human element of friendship that is necessary and a part of God's providential plan for our lives, both as His children but especially, as men of God.

However, there is a danger. Even as lucifer deceived a third of the angels with his reasoning by bringing God's righteousness and character into question, some relationships will take the same path. It is only as we uphold His righteousness in our lives as individual leaders and make clear to other leaders, through word and deed, our position on this truth, that these type of relationships that are after the flesh and not after the Spirit of God will not come near us. We must make the Lord our dread, not men. Because we love the praise of God more than the praise of men, our hearts are fixed on Him.

We must be men and women of Christendom who will not hesitate to stay in step with the word, even if it means to draw the line with those relationships that are after the flesh no matter how popular, how rich or how powerful. Our God is a consuming fire and He shall be our fear, not man.

> *Matt 5:23,24 Therefore if thou bring thy gift to the altar, and there rememberest that thy brother hath ought against thee; Leave there thy gift before the altar, and go thy way; first be reconciled to thy brother, and then come and offer thy gift.*

God is raising a standard in the hearts of His men who grace the pulpit.

No longer will unsettled differences and hidden grudges be accepted as the norm. The Spirit of the Living God will unify us, and it will come through vessels who confront relationships that are not built on the truth.

As ministers of the Gospel, we have failed to understand that if we have not done all that is within our ability to be in harmony with our co–laborers, God is going to deal with us individually and corporately.

Somehow, we have been beguiled into believing that it does not matter what "Minister Doe" thinks about us. We want to just proceed and do God's will. This is not spiritual maturity, nor does it reflect principles by which the kingdom of God operates.

We want to stand in the pulpits all across America and preach reconciliation to the lost, but we will not go across the street to be reconciled to our brother. In time, a little leaven will leaven your whole ministry. It will produce thorns and thistles rather than herbs.

125

One of the most shallow excuses that is practiced regarding differences in relationships among ministers is that they think God will work it out by His sovereignty. May the Lord show us the folly of our reasoning and the error of our way.

The demand that God has upon His ministers and all those who call upon His name has not changed. Though Paul did not consider himself among the elite and suffered much persecution because of his position, he still confronted the wrong in the church no matter what it cost him in terms of being rejected. Times have changed, but God's principles yet remain the same. You might cover the western hemisphere in church work, however, if you have ill relationships with people that you have not attempted to reconcile, you are preaching under the banner of hypocrisy. If you have wronged a man by not telling him his fault, you are robbing him of knowing the truth.

I am not suggesting that we be at peace with everyone just for the sake of peace. That is humanism. I am saying that we stand for truth and righteousness as God's representatives in all our dealings, in and out of the pulpit. This is the standard by which we are to live.

Church discipline is practically unheard of today. Why? Because many of our pastors are not enduring discipline themselves.

Matt 18:15–17 Moreover if thy brother shall trespass against thee, go and tell him his fault between thee and him alone: if he shall hear thee, thou hast gained thy brother. But if he will not hear thee, then take with thee one or two more, that in the mouth of two or three witnesses every word may be established. And if he shall neglect to hear them, tell it unto the church: but if he neglect to hear the church, let him be unto thee as an heathen man and a publican.

This is the very purging that the Body of Christ is headed for. Christians are tired of people acting like they love them while not hesitating to demonstrate an ungodly demeanor when the flesh is provoked for the most insignificant of reasons.

The obedient churches and ministers that experience the last day move of God are not going to tolerate relationships that are shallow and full of guile. They will simply and directly communicate:

"Brother or Sister, I sense in my spirit that something is wrong between you and I. Let us get together in righteousness in order to correct ourselves for God's glory. If I have done something to you, tell me. Or, if you have done something to me, I must tell you that I might be found upright before God."

The devil does not want godly relationships that are unified by the Spirit. He does not mind relationships of the flesh because they can do no harm against his kingdom. But those who walk with each other by the Spirit of God will put the enemy to flight and do great exploits for the Lord!

2 Cor 5:16 Wherefore henceforth know we no man after the flesh: yea, though we have known Christ after the flesh, yet now henceforth know we him no more.

God wants His body perfectly joined together in relationship and those who will abound in the fivefold ministry are going to begin to confront relationships that God may be glorified. If we are afraid of what people might say or do, then perhaps we have not been chosen. Yes, many are called, but those who are chosen are going to arise to the standard and not look back. They are going to proceed to the next level in God's plan for our generation along with the few who will not be hindered by relationships that do not meet God's approval which is upheld the standard of His holy Word.

Even in the midst of all the activity, fanfare and hoopla of ministries today, some will continue on without understanding God's timing for today. They will utter parables that are orchestrated by man. Even though God will work by His sovereignty to get what He wants out of such events, they will profit very little in eternity. What is of significance is relationship with God and my brother. This is what will last.

You see, those who have no self–interest have nothing to lose. They are free to speak the truth because they know that God will uphold them! We talk about power, faith, and all the gifts of the Spirit, but forgiveness and reconciliation is thrust behind fake dinners and shallow pats on the back while pursuing self interests.

Even those who are capable of being a blessing to other ministries have shut up their bowels of compassion due to vain philosophy that is built on fear. We avoid our ability to bless by judging and looking for fault.

> *1 John 3:17 But whoso hath this world's good, and seeth his brother have need, and shutteth up his bowels of compassion from him, how dwelleth the love of God in him?*

We seek the approval of another man and not the approval of God on that man. This mentality must be recognized as what it is: **128** REBELLION!

Though subtle and non–assuming, it is just that; rebellion. Why? Because we shy away from drawing closer to our Heavenly Father. Therefore, the need to be affirmed by others becomes a crux and eventually, a stumbling block to spiritual growth and development. Through seeking affirmation from men, we fail to be approved of God. Such are bastards in the pulpit who are preaching about a Father they themselves have refused to yield to. They are afraid, fearful and unbelieving in the very Bible they are holding in their own hands and the God they are declaring from the own mouths.

Many of today's young leaders have started ministries in the midst of shallow and weak relationships. They know how to teach on prophecy, but cannot write a letter back to their brother. They can fly to Africa to conduct a conference, but will not dial information to seek reconciliation. The truth is the truth and all else is a mirage that appears to be but is not.

Ministers who are avoiding depth of relationship surround themselves with weak men whom they can control, or with those who refuse to confront issues. This is wrong.

1 Tim 5:22 Lay hands suddenly on no man, neither be partaker of other men's sins: keep thyself pure.

Those who are moving on to glory have a fearless mind and a godly seriousness with righteousness and grace. They are tested to see if they are controllable or if they would present a challenge to the traditions of men. If they would take a stand, they would be classified as too serious, judgmental, or critical. In most situations, they have not been discerned by the Spirit but instead, judged by the flesh.

The truth of the matter is that those who are being possessed by *129* God are causing conviction in those who are drawing back. Without saying a word, the Spirit of God will emanate forth from such that walk with Him, and a person will recoil if their heart is not set on facing the truth which is in Christ Jesus.

I believe that many ministers are lacking the fullness of God in their ministry due to ministry related relationships that are after the flesh. However, all of the blame cannot be shifted to another. One must deal with the motives of their own heart. In order for the deception to work, there must be a greed element on both sides. The only way crooks can be in business is to find someone who wants something for nothing. There are many religious people who want the Christian experience without the Christian cross.

We must fulfill God's righteousness and not our own. If heaven is our only goal rather than what awaits us behind heaven's doors, we will do just enough to enter in with little or no works. Therefore, many will not reign in areas of high places of kingdom government in the life to come.

> *1 Cor 3:15 If any man's work shall be burned, he shall suffer loss: but he himself shall be saved; yet so as by fire.*

When all of our labors are finished and the Millennial Reign is completed, we will see the price we paid in avoiding these issues in our life. The decisions that we make today carry with them an eternal weight of judgment. It is God's purpose to stir Himself upon the earth and within the heavens. He is calling for His sons and daughters to confront their relationships that they may progress to a new level of glory.

As you close this book, reflect on the lives of the 11 disciples (and the apostle Paul) whom Jesus trained and scourged. He did not lose one disciple, except the son of perdition that the Scriptures might be fulfilled. Their lives are evidence of what occurs when men submit their lives and relationships to Him who holds all power and authority.

May we not shy away from the hand of God's correction. Instead, may we arise to upholding the character of the Lord in all of our affairs.

The Spirit of the Lord is visiting our pulpits, and all who are without chastisement will be found bastards. But I am hopeful that the love and conviction of God will attempt to penetrate the most callous heart that perhaps a glimmer of sorrow be found, and true repentance sought.

INSECURITIES

The reality of insecurities of those in the pulpit cannot be ignored. This fact can be attributed to many symptoms, yet shall we simply cut to the chase? There are those who moved forward in the vineyard of the Lord without a strong, tested, bonafide foundation in Christ Jesus. Your testimony is not a license for ministry. It merely glorifies what Christ has done, not what you can do.

The paradox of God working through men is profound indeed. We behold the move of God through vessels whom we deem above the commandment of God to produce fruit that reflects the life of God being lived as it is being declared. It is a commandment.

> *1 Ti 3:7 Moreover he must have a good report of them which are without; lest he fall into reproach and the snare of the devil.*

It is imperative that we build a real life in Christ Jesus that is not dependent upon the Body of Christ alone, but upon Christ Himself and then through Him; the Body of Christ. Without a doubt, our demanding of such fruit must be of a godly sort, but it must emphatically be a real part of our standard in relationships. If you are a bearer of God's word, please realize that the same word will cut you if you fail to stand for the whole truth. Remember, it is a doubled edge sword and will cut both ways.

I sincerely believe that the flattery of men and relationships that are after the flesh have proven to be the greatest snare to our commitment to God the Father. It was satan himself who wanted a relationship with God that he could not have. He wanted to be likened to the Son, but that glory was not going to be given him. Still today, the heart is yet seeking to receive glory and if one is not careful, they will attempt to take it from God. This is why the Spirit of the Lord is warning those who are in His vineyard to be real and be found with a genuine relationship with Him and your brother when He returns.

COVENANT RELATIONSHIPS

There is much talk today about "covenant relationships" in certain circles of Christianity. There must be caution in this area and I believe only the Scriptures can place proper perspective on this topic.

First of all, no one can establish a covenant relationship by themselves, for themselves and of themselves within the context of the Christian faith. Of course, if a person wants to establish a covenant by their own guidelines, they can do so by providing either blood or something of significant value to activate the promise of their covenant and the purpose for it. This was often done in the Old Testament (Gen. 21:27; 1 Sam. 18:3; 2 Sam. 5:3; 1 Kings 5:12; 20:34; Jer. 34:8). Certain Scriptures will support covenants between men or humans.

However, when covenants are established in the realm of Christianity, one must exercise caution that I will not speak lightly about. The covenant that I speak of is established upon the blood of Christ and upon promises that can only be secured by faith in the person who decreed it, namely God. His chosen representative is only qualified to enter into and accept those who come into this covenant relationship with Him; Jesus Christ.

> *Heb 8:10 For this is the covenant that I will make with the house of Israel after those days, saith the Lord; I will put my laws into their mind, and write them in their hearts: and I will be to them a God, and they shall be to me a people:*

> *Heb 12:24 And to Jesus the mediator of the new covenant, and to the blood of sprinkling, that speaketh better things than that of Abel.*

This is the Covenant of the New Testament that I speak of. The talk of covenant relationships today are seeking to bind men or women into relationships that are designed to obligate them to one another without regard to the binding relationship that they have with Christ.

In other words, as Christians, we are already in a covenant relationship with Christ. There is no need to be in another with our brother or sister who is in Christ as well. Further, to establish a covenant within a covenant is illegal for there cannot be two loyalties. This is why people must understand what a person means when they say, "I want to come into covenant with you." The only thing that can separate a covenant relationship is death. Nothing can separate us from Christ because He conquered death itself. This is why it is called the everlasting covenant.

> *Heb 13:20 Now the God of peace, that brought again from the dead our Lord Jesus, that great shepherd of the sheep, through the blood of the everlasting covenant,*

As I said earlier, there are covenants between people such as the covenant of marriage, the covenants of business relationships or the covenants of governments to name a few. However, when we speak of spiritual covenants, we must take heed and realize the ramifications of such relationships.

It was the scribes and Pharisees who ruled the Old Covenant under the law. This is why they hated Christ. Therefore, the sons of the scribes and Pharisees in today's dispensation will likewise seek to bind men into relationships that make them committed to them, not to Christ.

> *Col 2:8 Beware lest any man spoil you through philosophy and vain deceit, after the tradition of men, after the rudiments of the world, and not after Christ.*

It becomes clear throughout the whole thrust of religion that it is really about covenants. In conclusion on this issue, it should suffice all those who profess Christ to have fellowship with those who are one in Christ already by the blood of His covenant. We are to owe no man anything but love. To be required to give more than this is not necessary. Let our "yes" be "yes" and our "no" be "no." Anything more than this is evil.

The Epistle of James says that "the wisdom from above is first pure, then peaceable, gentle, and easy to be entreated, full of mercy and good fruits, without partiality, and without hypocrisy" (Jas 3:17). When we seek more than what we have in Christ's Covenant, we are seeking something of men that is not ours. We are being moved by a "wisdom that descendeth not from above, but is earthly, sensual, dev-ilish" (Jas 3:15).

No matter how close we might be to our brother, we are never closer to men that we are to Christ. I believe in supporting those in ministry. I believe in following leadership. I believe in heart to heart fellowship. However, as soon as a man no longer follows Christ, who alone is the mediator between God and man, nor will I follow that man. Remember, the heart is desperately wicked and only the Lord knows the heart and tries the reigns of it.

There is one way to determine if a person is in a covenant rela-tionship that is not based on Christ; they are very difficult to come out of it. There is a sense of control and manipulation and the free-dom to simply be free and to be moved of God as He would have it is not present. In short, there is no liberty.

> *Acts 17:28 For in him we live, and move, and have our being; as certain also of your own poets have said, For we are also his offspring.*

Christ has not called us to a yoke of bondage to be entangled again therein. We are called to a liberty that no man can regulate, no man can dictate, and no man can imitate.

> *Gal 5:1 Stand fast therefore in the liberty wherewith Christ hath made us free, and be not entangled again with the yoke of bondage.*

ONE MEDIATOR

Today's interpretation of covenant tends to make us think that if we are outside the relationship of certain people or organizations, we are unable to be used of God within His Body. Another necessary point on this subject is that when we discuss covenants with men, we must use caution. There is only one mediator necessary for us to access God and all other things that have been freely given us of Him. That mediator is Jesus Christ.

1 Ti 2:5 For there is one God, and one mediator between God and men, the man Christ Jesus;

When we recall previous generations and those that made monumental contributions to our spiritual heritage, they were seldom large groups of people. From Gideon to Martin Luther to missionaries that we know nothing of, God uses those that know Him and obey His will. They were in covenant with God and God alone. We are led to believe that the greatness of our size or the influence of our name moves mountains. It brings me pleasure to tell you that there is no good thing in man and without Christ, we can do nothing.

It appears that the Christian church is attempting to manage God's people like the Roman Catholic church. They see themselves as being God's spokesman, rather than Christ. Let us rest assured that Christ alone is our Mediator and that we can have confidence in knowing that we need not be compelled to pledge allegiance to men fearing that we will miss what God has for us. Nothing can separate me from the love of God that is in Christ Jesus. Yes… in Christ Jesus.

EXHORTATION

Lastly, I encourage all young men of God to arise to their call. Let no man despise your youth. Take heed to the ministry which you have received in the Lord and fulfill it, for in doing so, you shall snatch many from satan's grip and hell's doors, and usher them into the kingdom of light. Be an example of sons of God who walk in His nature by the Spirit and rebuke the devil with all authority. Respect men, but fear none for such is the snare of the heart.

Elders, leaders and all the fathers of the faith, I admonish you from my heart as a son, to uphold the whole counsel of God. Do not allow your labors to be unqualified in the last hours of time. May we all reject the rebellion of the heart and yield ourselves completely to God. May we endure the chastisement that He has decreed for us, knowing He does so for our good that we would be partakers of His holiness.

> *Heb 6:9 But, beloved, we are persuaded better things of you, and things that accompany salvation, though we thus speak. For God is not unrighteous to forget your work and labour of love, which ye have shewed toward his name, in that ye have ministered to the saints, and do minister.*

> *Heb 12:10-15 For they verily for a few days chastened us after their own pleasure; but he for our profit, that we might be partakers of his holiness. Now no chastening for the present seemth to be joyous, but grievous: nevertheless afterward it yieldeth the peaceable fruit of righteousness unto them which are exercised thereby. Wherefore lift up the hands which hang down, and the feeble knees; And make straight paths for your feet, lest that which is lame be turned out of the way; but let it rather be healed. Follow peace with all men, and holiness, without which no man shall see the Lord: Looking diligently lest any man fail of the grace of God; lest any root of bitterness springing up trouble you, and thereby many be defiled;*

Come quickly Lord Jesus; Come quickly. Amen.

137

Make your plans to attend the upcoming stage
production play in Raleigh, NC!
For more information, visit our official site:
www.bastardsinthepulpit.com

Please review exciting books written by the Owens Family
Published by:
Higher Standard Publisher.

Purchase our Ebooks online and save over 50%!

You may order and inquire on-line at

www.higherstandardpublishers.com

Divine Protocol - The Order of God's Kingdom
By William Owens

Lays a foundation to help you grow towards spiritual maturity. This powerful book deals with family, ministry, prayer, dealing with demons, mandates, being single and a host of relevent issues regarding the Kingdom of God. You will be challenged as you mature in the things of God.

270 pages $24.95 ISBN 0-9658629-4-1   Ebook only $8.95

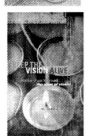

Keep the Vision Alive: Make,
Don't Break, the Man of Vision
By Selena Owens

When God has placed a visionary in your life, there are experiences that will make you or break you. Mrs. Owens is very familiar with working with a visionary and in this book, she brings to the forefront the call of wives to empower their husbands in fulfilling the vision. *Topics include: Characteristics of a Man of Vision, Understanding the Vision, Selfishness, Pride, Prayer, Support, A Time to Sow. Workbook included inside of book.*

108 pages $11.95 ISBN: 0-9-658629-3-3   Ebook only $4.95

Helpmeet: The Power to Help Your Husband
By Selena Owens

Learn the wisdom of how a wife helps her husband the way God has ordained and decreed.

134 pages $11.95 ISBN 0-9658629-1-7   Ebook only $4.95

Wisdom: The Principal Thing: Get It!
by William Owens

The generation of our young people need wisdom. Without wisdom, the decisions necessary to secure a powerful life as an young adult will be impossible. A verse by verse commentary on Proverbs 8. It will both bless and challenge the young adult.

67 pages $6.95 ISBN 0-9658629-8-4   Ebook only $3.95

Heartbeat: Inspirational Short Stories
From God's Heart to Yours
by Tiffany Owens
17 years young

Writing since the age of seven, 16-year-old Tiffany Owens is inspired by her walk with Jesus Christ and the world around her. Heartbeat are three short stories that are written to inspire the readers heart to grow closer to God. It takes the practical issues of everyday life and compels us to see the love and power of God at work in bringing us nearer His heart.

146 pages $9.95   Ebook only $4.95

Printed in the United States
45532LVS00005B/163-201

WHEN CHURCH LEADERSHIP REJECTS THE FATHERHOOD OF GOD...

WHY IT HAPPENS
HOW IT AFFECTS
OUR FAMILIES
and
HOW TO DEAL WITH IT.

Exposing the problem of bastards in the pulpit is not a choice as servants of God. Rather, it is a mandate, an irrevocable order, a command bearing weight of responsibility that extends into eternity. It is time for the Body of Christ to boldly identify the difference between one who has been purged from self-interests, political agendas, fear of faces, and hidden sins, even to one who justifies his sins because of grace. In these days of increasing apostasy, we must realize there are sons and then there are bastards...in the pulpit.

The Stage Production
Summer 2006 • Raleigh, NC

BASTARDS
in the **pulpit**

For more information visit: www.bastardsinthepulpit.com

William Owens is a prolific author of nine books dealing with Christian maturity and spiritual warfare. He has also completed his first playwrite for stage, "Bastards in the Pulpit." The mandate on his life is to uphold the standard of God's Word throughout the Body of Christ and bring a radical message of salvation to those who are lost. William and his wife Selena, have been married for 20 years and have four children. They reside in Raleigh, NC.

HIGHER STANDARD
PUBLISHERS

www.higherstandardpublishers.com

U.S. $ 14.99
ISBN 0-9658629-0-9
514
9 780965 862905